For
Edgar

Acknowledgments

For their unflagging interest, inspiring guidance, and wise suggestions I owe a debt of gratitude to Dr. Caroline Robbins and Dr. Arthur Dudden of Bryn Mawr College that can never be repaid.

I am also indebted to Dr. Nicholas B. Wainwright of the Historical Society of Pennsylvania for introducing me to Phineas Bond and for placing at my disposal the valuable Bond Collection and other important manuscripts owned by the Society. I wish also to thank the Controller of Her Majesty's Stationary Office for permission to examine and make use of Crown-copyright material in the Public Record Office and Mrs. Morris-Davies of Oxford, England for allowing me to study the Burges Papers at the Bodleian Library.

To the many people who in large and small measure contributed to this book may I say, "Thank you."

Preface

Seven years of war forced a reluctant mother country to recognize the independence of the thirteen American colonies. With the signing of the treaty at Paris on the 3rd of September 1783, the rebellion came to a formal end, and a new state entered the family of nations. But the resulting peace stopped short of men's minds and spirits. There was no binding up of wounds nor forgetting of past injuries.

On the contrary, hatred persisted and, if anything, intensified. On both sides of the Atlantic a nurturing of grievances, of suspicions, and of jealousies continued. For over thirty years Britons and Americans viewed one another with a jaundiced eye until a second peace treaty—this time at Ghent in 1814—brought to a formal close a second Anglo-American war.

In the midst of this long, drawn-out conflict moved Phineas Bond, Esq. He reached the age of reason in Philadelphia before the outbreak of the War for Independence and was politically active in Pennsylvania from the beginning of what he called, "the Time of Troubles." He played a role as an American Tory, albeit a brief one, in the Revolution itself and with thousands of other Loyalists sought asylum in England. During a seemingly endless exile he became one of the most trusted attorneys of those British merchants in the Atlantic trade to whom Americans owed vast sums of money. Three years after the Peace of Paris, Bond returned to Philadelphia as His Britannic Majesty's consul to the middle states and as a representative of the merchants. There he remained, serving king and traders, until the eve of the War of 1812.

Although occupying comparatively minor posts, Bond became a microcosm of his time. His thoughts and work, his dreams and hopes, his experiences and convictions point up the era between the two wars for American independence.

He expressed much of general British feeling toward the

United States. Never able to appreciate fully what the new country had to offer, he sensed its potential strengths. Until the end of his days he remained in his inner being—as did many of his country-men—fundamentally afraid of the infant nation.

As an agent of His Majesty's government, he reflected the changing attitudes and policies of the British ministries toward the United States. At the beginning of his tour, his experiences illuminate their stumbling search for a suitable means of reestablishing relations. For the first five years of his consular career, Anglo-American diplomatic connections were largely nonexistent and Bond attempted to fill the vacuum. Once relations were regularized, his work with the first ministers plenipotentiary sheds light on the tortuous route leading to a rapprochement between the two countries and upon the difficulties, if not impossibilities, of maintaining "Harmony and Good Understanding" in the midst of world conflict.

The opening of the titanic wars of the French Revolution altered the nature of his duties. He became a spy, a policeman, and more than ever a champion of his country's interests. He had to deal with the problems arising from American neutrality, with privateers and French convoys, with impressment and the stopping and searching of vessels of the United States on the high seas. Always evaluating cases and events from the point of view of an archmercantilist, an unrepentant Loyalist, and a devoted subject of the king, he obliges us to look upon the familiar and traditional in new lights.

His efforts on behalf of the British merchants introduce us to their distress and to their despair. They emerge not as greedy capitalists, sucking the lifeblood from the southern planter and the overextended New England debtor, but as the helpless victims that they were of revolution and circumstances beyond their control.

Finally, through Bond the story of an institution unfolds. For his history is that of the British consular service in the late eighteenth century and particularly of its origins, growth, and development in the United States of America.

Contents

Abbreviations Used in the Notes

AHAAR	*Annual Report of the American Historical Association*
AHR	*American Historical Review*
APS	American Philosophical Society
ASP,FR	*American State Papers, Foreign Relations*
BSP	*British Sessional Papers*
BT	Board of Trade
CAD COLL	Cadwalader Collection
CAD COLL, PB	Cadwalader Collection, Phineas Bond Section
FO	Foreign Office
HSP	Historical Society of Pennsylvania
PMHB	*Pennsylvania Magazine of History and Biography*
PRO	Public Record Office

PHINEAS BOND

CHAPTER ONE

The Return
of a Loyalist

Late Saturday afternoon, the 18th of November 1786, the New York stage rolled to a stop before the sign of the Indian Queen on Fourth Street in Philadelphia. It was the end of the daily run. All the passengers got off, among them a man in his middle thirties. He had been traveling since three o'clock that morning, when he boarded the ferry at New York City, and he was very tired.[1]

But in spite of his weariness he carried himself well. And his clothes—the wig, the beaver hat, the fluted-silver buckles beneath the knees and on the shoes, the broadcloth suit cut by a foreign tailor in the latest fashion—set him apart from the crowd milling around the tavern. His dress was so obviously that of a gentleman.

His nose, too, was aristocratic; long and pointed and cold-looking. Yet the eyes offset it; they were warm, and so was the mouth which was full and mobile and always seemed on the verge of breaking into a smile.

From the Indian Queen the man made his way east to Third Street and then south to Union Street where there were no stores and the few houses were separated one from another by lawns and gardens. There he turned left. He kept to the north side of Union Street until he came to the old Barclay place next to Campholler's Alley. It was a two-story, red-brick house—typical of Philadelphia —and had a large garden, carefully screened against the coming cold.[2] Mrs. Williamina Bond owned the house now. The man entered. After eight years of exile Phineas Bond had come home.

The ladies were waiting for him: Mrs. Bond, who so often had been afraid she would never again see her son, and Phineas' four sisters; Williamina, a widow with two children of her own; Rebecca, still a spinster; Elizabeth and Frances who had been school girls when they last saw their brother.

Happiness must have filled the house and perhaps there were even a few tears of joy. For once again the family had a head; the ladies, a "male Protector." Then too Bond had brought presents for everyone. There were gewgaws from Moore's jewelry shop on Ludgate Street in London and yards and yards of calico from the Malabar coast for dancing dresses.

The news of the return spread. Friends like the Allens and the Shippens, the Rawles and the Shoemakers, were delighted to learn Phineas was back. The small British colony in Philadelphia was also pleased. The doors opened when Bond called. One English lady, Ann Warder, was so captivated by Bond's easy manners that she noted his visit in her diary. When Mr. Bond called, she confessed, she had been in her morning dress and had apologized "for being such a figure at that time of day." With a low bow Bond replied that "he always thought a fine English woman a good figure."[3]

At 318 High Street they too looked forward to seeing Bond. Benjamin Franklin lived there. He had known the Bonds before Phineas was born; he had watched the boy grow; and for the past months Franklin had been apprised of the imminent return. He had heard from the eleventh earl of Buchan who had written that Phineas Bond, a relative by marriage, and "one of the worthiest and best men . . . is setting out for America."[4]

When Bond called at 318 High Street, he took gifts to the "great old man," English newspapers and pamphlets, and books for the American Philosophical Society. He also brought for "Mr. F's" amusement Debrett's latest piece of "trash," *Asylum for Fugitive Pieces.* Bond thought Franklin would find "some pleasant Things" in it, but would "soon discover the Book to be unfit for the Inspection of any of his fair Friends: unless," as Bond pointed out, Franklin "should exercise his Discretion in selecting such Parts as may be calculated to merit the Delicacy and Refinement of their Taste and to spare the Blush of *Prudery*."[5]

Within a few days it seemed as though all Philadelphia knew

Bond was back. Each of the public prints carried the news. The *Pennsylvania Packet and Daily Advertiser* went so far as to box the announcement in a black frame and set it in the center of the front page. The item fairly leapt at the reader when he opened the paper. It read in part:

> Last Saturday arrived in this city from London PHINEAS BOND, ESQUIRE, his Britannic majesty's consul for the states of New York, New Jersey, Pennsylvania, Delaware and Maryland, and commissary for commercial affairs within the dominions of the United States.[6]

While the news delighted those who lived around Union Street, in the Society Hill section of the city, it shocked most Philadelphians. The average resident remembered only too well who Phineas Bond was and what he had done in 1777. It seemed unbelievable he would dare return. Why, ran the gossip, if Bond had come back without the fancy titles he would be mounting the ladder to the gallows. Even in that city devoted to tolerance there were men who would with pleasure have watched Bond swing.

There was a similar reaction throughout the United States. The appointment struck the New York City merchants as highly "inappropriate." Bond, they argued, besides being "obnoxious to the Community at large, was bred to the law" and in their own words, "is unacquainted with our Commerce." They predicted that "the best treatment he can expect to meet with is public Insult & private contempt from all Ranks of People."

One of the merchants was so angered by the commissioning of Bond that he tried to scotch it. He wrote a blistering letter to Sir George Yonge, who had been British secretary of war. The trader emphasized how disliked Bond was in America and suggested it would be best were he recalled. "We are the Compleatest and most Enterprising Merchants this side of the Equator," read the letter, "no Laws you can pass, or the severest Restrictions you can Establish, can restrain us, we have now British Ships, British Registers, British Certificates, British Oaths Authenticated with British Seals . . . You should have appointed a Man of Business."[7]

Americans pointed to the selection of Bond as another example of the perfidy of Albion, as another grievance to add to the growing list. The frontier was bleeding and the Indians, it was said, were firing with flintlocks made in Britain. The British refused to negotiate a commercial treaty with the United States. They had shut the West Indies and the Maritime Provinces to American shipping. Although America had sent one of her finest citizens, John Adams, to London as minister, no ambassador had as yet arrived from Great Britain. Instead the government had sent Phineas Bond. They had given "a Bond for an Adams!" The exchange appeared unfavorable.[8]

In Virginia Governor Edmund Randolph heard about Bond's arrival from Edward Carrington who was a member of the Continental Congress. Carrington connected the appointment with "this mischievous affair," as he worded it, "in Massachusetts." There the debtors were revolting under the leadership of Daniel Shays, and in Carrington's opinion Britain was fomenting the rebellion. She is keeping herself "in readiness," wrote Carrington, "to improve any advantage which our derangements may present for regaining her lost dominions." Every appointment, including Mr. Bond's, is "calculated to this object." But, continued the letter, Bond's reception "remains to be contemplated. I trust that I shall never harbour unreasonable jealousies, but when we know that an invidious foe, is vested with the garb of peace and friendship, it behooves us to be Vigilant. . . ."[9]

As a member of Virginia's delegation to the Continental Congress, Carrington's thoughts on the appointment carried weight. For Congress would decide whether to recognize Bond as British consul and commissary or whether to vote down his appointments. Yet in the final analysis the vote would hinge upon the recommendations of John Jay, America's foreign secretary. And Jay, too, was contemplating Mr. Bond's credentials.

On the foreign secretary's desk lay the commissions together with reports from the American embassy in London. One of the dispatches advocated extreme caution with respect to Bond's appointments. It read in part as follows:

> I do not think it improbable, after they [i.e., the British] establish as many Consuls as they think will answer their ends, those Gentlemen, if not closely attended to, will be found coming

gently forward, with separate proposals to the States or districts where they may respectively reside, for the establishment of a commercial intercourse independent of Federal systems; and thus, by holding out separate advantageous plans to the several States, they expect it will be unnecessary to trouble Congress and our Federal Government on the subject.[10]

In other words, Great Britain planned through Bond and others to divide and reconquer the lost colonies.

Thus, in the last months of 1786, it was uncertain whether Phineas Bond would remain in Philadelphia protected by the law of nations, or whether he would be arrested and imprisoned, or whether he must again flee into exile.

NOTES

[1]See stagecoach advertisements in the *Pennsylvania Gazette* for 1786; July and August 1788; Rufus Wilmot Griswold, *The Republican Court in the Days of Washington* (New York, 1856), p. 117.

[2]Record of Deeds, County of Philadelphia, City Hall, Philadelphia, Pennsylvania, D 41, 130–131.

[3]Ann Warder, "Extracts from the Diary of Ann Warder," Sarah Cadbury, ed., *The Pennsylvania Magazine of History and Biography,* XVIII (Philadelphia, 1894), 56, 63.

[4]Lord Buchan to Benjamin Franklin, Edinburgh, September 3, 1786, Letters to Dr. Franklin, The American Philosophical Society, Philadelphia, Pennsylvania, XXXIV, 139.

[5]Phineas Bond to Franklin, Union Street, June 4, 1787, Franklin Letters, APS, XXXV, 72.

[6]Tuesday, November 21, 1786; see also *Pennsylvania Gazette,* November 22, 1786.

[7]Anonymous merchant to Sir George Yonge, New York, December 6, 1786, Foreign Office Records, Public Record Office, London, England, FO 4/4.

[8]See Samuel Flagg Bemis, *Jay's Treaty, A Study in Commerce and Diplomacy* (New York, 1924), pp. 10–19; A. L. Burt, *The United States, Great Britain and British North America from the Revolution to the Establishment of Peace after the War of 1812* (New Haven, 1940), pp. 91–104.

[9]Edward Carrington to Edmund Randolph, New York, December 8, 1786, *Letters of Members of the Continental Congress,* Edmund C. Burnett, ed. (Washington, D.C., 1936), VIII, 518; see also Rufus King to John Adams, New York, May 4, 1786, *Ibid.,* VIII, 353.

[10]W. S. Smith to John Jay, London, September 4, 1786, *Diplomatic Correspondence of the United States of America, from the Signing of the Definitive Treaty of Peace, to the Adoption of the Constitution* (Washington, D.C., 1873), III, 47.

CHAPTER TWO

Youth

In America, the Bonds were an old and distinguished family. Originally from Bury St. Edmunds in West Suffolk, England, they emigrated during the civil wars. Two sons of Thomas Bond arrived in Massachusetts Bay Colony in 1642. Three years later their eldest brother, Thomas, pulled up stakes and crossed the Atlantic. He settled in Maryland, pursued his profession, which was medicine, bought a plantation in Calvert County, acquired a number of slaves, and established a family that is extant.

Upon his death the Calvert County plantation went to his son, Richard. He added to the acreage of the estate, farmed, and presumedly lived the life of a typical eighteenth century Maryland planter. Richard Bond married a distant kinswoman who bore him five sons.[1] Two, Thomas and Phineas, elected to follow in their grandfather's footsteps and to become doctors. Since there were no medical schools in North America, when they came of age the boys went to Europe.

Thomas studied surgery in London and Paris. Phineas earned degrees in general medicine from the University of Rheims and from the University of Leyden.[2] By the early 1740's both had returned to America, but not to Maryland. They set up practice in Philadelphia. The fast-growing town with its intellectual groups and cosmopolitan atmosphere had much to offer well-educated and ambitious young men. Seizing their opportunities, the Bonds quickly established themselves as civic and professional figures of importance.

Thomas almost immediately upon arrival obtained the position of quarantine physician for the port of Philadelphia. In 1745,

Phineas became a member of City Council. a post that he held until his death. Doctors with European degrees were scarce, even in Philadelphia. As a result, the practice of the Bonds flourished. The brothers looked upon it as a copartnership. They used the same daybooks and seldom troubled to indicate who had answered the calls that were carefully itemized together with the prescriptions recommended and the fees charged. The names of the Bonds's patients read like a list of the "first persons" of the city: the Shoemakers and the Norrises, the Chews and the Galloways, the Kidds, the Purveyances, and the Franklins.[3] Many of the patients also became friends of the doctors.

They were particularly close to John Bartram and Thomas Godfrey, to William Parsons and Samuel Rhodes, and to Benjamin Franklin; to the men who were transforming Philadelphia into the cultural center of North America. As might be expected, the Bonds also became founders of institutions.

Both Phineas and Thomas helped establish the Philadelphia Assembly, the Society of the Sons of St. George, the American Philosophical Society, the City College—which became the present University of Pennsylvania—and the Pennsylvania Hospital, the first of its kind in the American colonies. In short, the Bonds became leaders of Philadelphia society.[4]

In 1748, one of the social events of the year occurred when Dr. Phineas Bond married Miss Williamina Moore, granddaughter of the fourth earl of Wemyss and daughter of Judge William Moore, potentate of Chester County. The wedding took place on the 4th of August at Moore Hall, just north of Valley Forge.[5] After the ceremonies the couple moved to Philadelphia.

On July 15, 1749, Williamina Moore Bond gave birth to a male child. Nine days later at Christ's Church the infant was baptized and christened Phineas after his father.

The early years of Phineas Bond remain clouded in obscurity. He was, we know, raised as an Episcopalian. When old enough he probably sat in the family pew at Christ's Church and listened to the sermons of his uncle, the Rev. William Smith.[6] He may even have attended his uncle's Academy. Whatever his primary education, Bond was bred to be a gentleman.

He learned manners, and so well that throughout life a bow or a finely turned phrase came to him as second nature. The values of a gentleman, the responsibilities as well as the privileges, became part of him. A gracious house, servants, a good table, vintage wine, elegant clothes must for Bond always be maintained no matter what the cost. But, so too must loyalty to the family and personal integrity.

At fourteen, Phineas Bond entered the City College. It could hardly have been otherwise since one uncle, William Smith, was provost, another uncle, Thomas Bond, was a founder and his own father was a trustee. Bond proved to be bright; he completed the requirements for graduation in three years and in the spring of 1766 received the degree of Bachelor of Arts.[7] He was then seventeen and had his heart set on becoming a lawyer.

The selection must have disappointed his father; there were no other boys to whom he could leave his practice, Phineas was the only son. Yet it seemed as though he was more under the influence of his grandfather than his father. The judgeship, Moore Hall, the baronetcy, the family titles had left their mark. Then too a strong mutual affection existed between the old man and young Bond. He was the first grandchild and the only one whom William Moore named in his will. In that document the judge called Phineas "Worthy" and left him, in Moore's own words, "all my Law books as a token of my love and regard for him."[8]

And so Bond was apprenticed to the bar in Philadelphia. When he reached twenty-one, his father agreed he should complete his legal studies at the Middle Temple in London.

Bond prepared for the trip. He collected letters of introduction. Two were to Franklin; one from Joseph Galloway. The great lawyer recommended Bond to Franklin's "advice and Friendship," because of his "particular Regard for his Parents" and because of Bond's excellent conduct during his apprenticeship. Galloway added that he was confident young Bond "will prove neither ingrateful, or unworthy of any Favors you shall confer upon him."[9] Mrs. Franklin, using her own inimitable spelling, authored the second letter. It read as follows:

MY DEAR CHILD
   the bairer of this is the Son of Dr. Phinis Bond his only son and a worthey young man he is a going to studey the Law he desired a line to you I beleve you have such a number of worthey young Jentelmen as ever wente to gather I hope to give you pleshuer to see such a numbe of fine youthes from your own countrey which will be an Honour to that parentes and countrey.
   I am my Dear child your ffeckshonot
wife   D. FRANKLIN

   1770
ocktober the 11[10]

On October 18, 1770, Bond sailed from Chester on the *Britannia*. She was a new ship and that was all to the good. For she was only two days out when she ran into a northeaster. The winds were of gale force; the mainsails split; the ship threatened to founder; in order to save her Captain Falconer was obliged to have part of the cargo thrown overboard.[11] The danger finally passed, and Bond arrived safely in London. Nevertheless, months later he was still talking about the storm, confessing how badly frightened he had been, and as a result had developed, in his own words, "a pretty tolerable aversion to this mode of travelling."

But by then he had fallen in love "with this precious stone set in a silver sea." He thought London the finest city in the world. He adored the sights and the sounds . . . the old Jezebel he saw on his way to Commons who surely had turned eighty and "had diamonds on her head to the value of several thousands" . . . the stillness in the courtyards of Middle Temple . . . the lack of supervision . . . "A Templar," wrote Bond, "keeps what hours he pleases, has no one to call him to account for any malpractices he may be guilty of beyond the Breach of Peace."[12]

Yet Bond found the going rough. Good as his preparation had been as an American, it was by no means equivalent to that of other Templars. It became his conviction that nothing surpassed an English public school education. Bond envied those who had the benefit of such training. He wished he had come to London years earlier. As a colonial he must put in five years at a hall before he could be called to the bar, but if he had graduated from Oxford, instead of the City College in Philadelphia, only three years would be required.[13]

Hard as Bond was obliged to work, he found time to handle cases. In 1772, for instance, he collected for Thomas Wagetuff, a London jeweler, the sum of £53-2-0 sterling owed by Jonathan Potts of Reading, Pennsylvania for purchases made in 1768. Neate & Pigou, one of the largest merchant houses trading to the middle colonies, engaged Bond to represent them in cases where Americans owed money. At the same time Bond became associated with the house of Crafton & Colson. He proved so effective in collecting debts that Richard Crafton advised the company's general attorney in America to use Phineas Bond, Esq. "in all Matters . . . that may require the Assistance of a Lawyer."[14] Thus while studying, Bond laid the foundations for his future practice. The pattern of his life appeared to be already fixed.

Then, in the spring of 1773, Bond received word that he must return home immediately; his father was very ill. Without completing his studies, Bond was obliged to leave England. At the beginning of May, he was in Philadelphia.[15]

He found his father failing fast and tormented by the realization that he had never made a will. Bond promised to right that situation and at once drew up a bequest. The document, in accordance with Dr. Bond's wishes, left everything to his wife. But by the time it was completed, Dr. Bond was delirious; he never recovered sufficiently to sign the will. In the middle of June, Dr. Phineas Bond died.[16]

At twenty-four his son was presented with a ready-made family. Bond became responsible for his mother and his five, unmarried sisters. The eldest, named for her mother, was just twenty. There followed Anne, Rebecca, Elizabeth, and Frances. It was a large family for a young man. But without complaint Bond threw himself into the role of "male Protector." He worked extremely hard at his profession, gained additional accounts, and by 1776 was earning an average of £600 sterling a year—roughly £900 in Pennsylvania currency.[17] Bond was justifiably pleased.

He was also occupied with the probate of his father's estate. Having died without a will, all property had to be inventoried and transformed into liquid assets. Even Sheffield, the doctor's personal slave, must be sold; all debts must be paid; back accounts must be collected from a shockingly long list of patients; and bonds and land holdings must be cashed.[18] When the estate was finally cleared, the family inherited around £7000 Pennsylvania currency; a considerable sum, which Bond augmented by abandoning all claims to the estate and formally transmitting his shares to his mother.[19] The inheritance together with Bond's earnings placed the family in comfortable circumstances.

Meanwhile Bond was becoming increasingly involved in political affairs. The tea ship *Polly* was on her way to Philadelphia. Later he looked back upon her arrival as marking, in his own words, "the Commencement of the Troubles." It was when his own thoughts on government and empire crystallized. There was no question in his mind that the British Empire was the finest in the world, offering to those within its confines incomparable benefits and opportunities. He was himself enormously proud of his British citizenship. Since from the time he was a little boy it had been hammered into him that obligations go hand in hand with privileges, he never doubted that the colonists ought to contribute to the defense of the empire. But, he insisted, Americans should be permitted to raise the revenue "in their own way." While parliament possessed the right to tax the provinces, it was, he claimed, "inexpedient" of that body to exercise the right.

In the local taverns and meeting places Bond made no secret of his views. He publicly avowed his opposition to the Tea Act and was equally vocal in denouncing the activities in Boston. Abhorring violence, as he did, and regarding the sanctity of property and the maintenance of law and order as the keystones of civilized society, it seemed to him that destroying the tea offered no solution to the problem. Time, an amiable atmosphere, and logically worded petitions were the requirements for resolving the disagreements. Given those conditions, he saw no reason why a constitutional compact could not be entered into between the two countries allowing the colonists to tax themselves.

When the *Polly* arrived, some eight thousand citizens gathered in the State House yard. Bond, among others, addressed the crowd, advocating moderation and recommending that the captain turn his ship around and sail for home with his full cargo, intact and unimpaired. Captain Ayres acted upon the suggestions. For the moment the endeavors of what Bond called "the Peaceable part of the Citizens" had succeeded.

People then thought of Bond as being somewhat Whiggish. But with the passing of the intolerable acts and the call from New York for a provincial congress, he moved to the extreme right. An assembly of the colonies under present conditions struck him as an overt and illicit action that would permanently tear the fabric of amicability. Equally menacing was the possibility that such a group might fall under the domination of the radicals. Bond helped form a committee of those who shared his views, drew up a remonstrance against the summoning of a continental congress, and canvassed the city and the surrounding counties for signatures. He was, in his own words, "defeated by the Violent Party" and henceforth "was himself advertized as Tory."[20]

He continued to work for "good sense" and in the local elections campaigned on behalf of the conservative candidates. In May 1775, Bond went so far as to join the Philadelphia militia in order to influence "the lowest of the People"·and to counteract "the Current which then ran greatly against the Tories." He became a private in Capt. John Little's company, second battalion. The enlisted men took to him; they elected him ensign and many voted Tory.[21]

But after the declaration of independence Bond withdrew from the militia. "From that time," as he later put it, "he positively refused even in Appearance to fall in with the Measures of the Insurgents and violently reprobated all their Measures."[22] He refused to take the oath of allegiance to the new United States of North America and was so open in his denunciations of independence that he gained a widespread reputation for being an enemy of freedom, a diehard Tory, and a supporter of the tyrant, George III.

By August of 1777, Bond found himself in an untenable position. With the threat of a British landing in Maryland, the American congress moved against the Loyalists and directed the state executives to round up all persons "who have in their General Conduct and Conversation evidenced a disposition inimical to the Cause of America." On Sunday, August 31, 1777, the Supreme Executive Council of Pennsylvania ordered that twenty-seven Tories, including Phineas Bond, be placed on parole. They must give their word of honor in writing "to remain in their Dwellings, ready to appear on the Demand of Council, and meanwhile to refrain from doing anything injurious to the United Free States."[23]

On Tuesday, three officers called at the Bond's house on the north side of Chestnut Street between Second and Third Streets. They presented Bond with the parole. At once he demanded to know the charge. "It ought to be of a very serious nature, indeed," declared Bond, "to warrant so extraordinary Proceedings." Moreover, did the officers realize that the situation failed to apply to him: that he was personally innocent? For no matter what his sentiments on public affairs, never had he—and this was a questionable statement—promulgated them "with a view of making Proselytes." The whole business struck him as highly irregular. Had it not been for the ladies, he would never have signed.[24] But for the peace of the family Bond begrudgingly consented to the terms of the parole.

When, however, Council refused to enlarge the limits, Bond declared himself no longer bound by the pledge and defiantly dared Council to do their worst. "I shall on no account whatsoever," read Bond's letter to the executives, "conceal or withdraw myself: neither shall I in any Respect attempt to elude the search and inquiry of those who without assigning any cause, aim at restraining that Liberty, which as a free man, I hold myself indisputably entitled to." At eight o'clock on the third of September, Phineas Bond found himself in jail, confined with twenty-one other Loyalists in the Free Mason's Lodge. Council had accepted the challenge.[25]

During the following days the prisoners busied themselves drawing up lengthy remonstrances. They protested to everyone they could think of: to the Council, to the president of the Council, to the United States Congress, and to the citizens of Pennsylvania. For the latter document Bond was largely responsible. "An Address to the Inhabitants of Pennsylvania" alleged that the "Free Mason" prisoners had been arrested without warrants and had been jailed *"unaccused and unheard."* No citizen, the remonstrance warned, remains secure. "Your homes," read the article, "which . . . are your castles against invaders, your chambers, your closets, your desks . . . your letters . . . are permitted to be broken, searched, exposed to the prying eye of malignant curiosity, and all without any well founded cause of suspicion."[26]

But the petitions failed to move Council. On Thursday, September 4, 1777, it was decided to send the Loyalists to Staunton, Virginia where they could cause little, if any, harm. Now, Bond acted. A message begging for help reached his uncle, Dr. Thomas Bond. As surgeon of the Continental Army, there was no question about the doctor's patriotism. When he appealed to Council on behalf of his errant nephew, Dr. Thomas' words made an impression. On Wednesday, September the 10th, Council resolved to grant Phineas Bond, Esq. another parole: he could go to Virginia and from there to the West Indies.[27]

On the next day, at three o'clock in the afternoon, wagons to carry the prisoners south arrived in the alley behind the lodge. Col. Nicola entered the building and read the names of those to go. Bond's name was off the list. He, therefore, refused to move. Col. Nicola, pressed for time as he was, failed to check. He took the line of least resistance and ordered Bond to remain in his, Nicola's, personal custody.[28] But once again Bond broke parole. Sometime during the following weeks, he managed to elude Nicola and made his way to the British lines.

On September 26, 1777, General William Howe's army was ready to occupy Philadelphia. Sophia Logan Fisher, a Loyalist at heart, rose early that morning to watch the sight. That evening in her diary she wrote as follows:

> About ten o'clock, the troops began to enter. The town was still, not a cart or any obstruction in the way. The morning had before been cloudy, but nearly the time of their entrance the sun shone out with a sweet serenity. . . . First came the light horses, led along by Enoch Story and Phineas Bond, as the soldiers were unacquainted with the town and the different streets, nearly two hundred I imagine in number, clean dress and their bright swords glittering in the sun.[29]

Bond had crossed his Rubicon. There could be no turning back. For, as the President of Pennsylvania put it in attainting Phineas Bond for high treason, he had "knowingly and willingly aided and assisted the enemies of this State and of the United States of America."[30]

When General Howe evacuated Philadelphia in June of 1778, Bond had no choice but to leave too. He went to New York City and then to England, leaving behind in Philadelphia his mother and five sisters.

NOTES

[1]See *American Ancestry: Giving the Name & Descent in the Male Line of Americans whose Ancestors Settled in the United States Previous to the Declaration of Independence* (Albany, 1890), V, 631; Christ's Church Genealogical Records, Genealogical Society of Pennsylvania, Philadelphia, Pennsylvania.

[2]By kindness of Elizabeth H. Thomson, Department of History of Science and Medicine, Yale University.

[3]See Copartnership Daybooks of Drs. Thomas and Phineas Bond, 1751–1767, Library of the College of Physicians, Philadelphia, Pennsylvania.

[4]See unpubl. ms. by Dr. Thomas R. Quinan, "Sketch of the Bonds," Cadwalader Collection, Dr. C. E. Cadwalader Section, Historical Society of Pennsylvania, Philadelphia, Pennsylvania, "Misc." Box.

[5]For the most authoritative account of Moore Hall see unpubl. ms. by Nicholas Wainwright, "Moore Hall, 1694–1794," HSP. Although reconditioned, the house still stands and retains some of the elegance it once possessed.

[6]The Bonds were raised as Quakers, and they joined the Philadelphia Friends when they took up residence in the city. But in July 1748, Dr. Phineas Bond was read out of meeting for "entering into war preparations." Philadelphia Friends Monthly Meeting Records, The Genealogical Society of Pennsylvania, VIII, 263 and IX, 245; "Notes on Friends Meetings," CAD COLL, Dr. C. E. Cadwalader Section, "Misc." Box. The Moores, on the other hand, were Church of England. Before her marriage Williamina worshipped with her parents at the St. Davids Church, in Radnor, Pennsylvania.

[7]Thomas Harrison Montgomery, *A History of the University of Pennsylvania from its Foundation to AD 1770 including Biographical Sketches of the Trustees, Faculty, the First Alumni and Others* (Philadelphia, 1900), *passim*.

[8]CAD COLL, Phineas Bond Section, "Moore" Box.

[9]Joseph Galloway to Franklin, Philadelphia, October 12, 1770, CAD COLL, PB, "B-W" Box.

[10]"Letters of Phineas Bond, British Consul at Philadelphia to the Foreign Office of Great Britain," J. Franklin Jameson, ed. *Annual Report of the American Historical Association for the Year 1896* (Washington, 1897), I, 514.

[11]See *Pennsylvania Packet & General Advertiser,* October 18, 1770, and *Pennsylvania Gazette,* November 8, 1770.

[12]Bond to Daniel Clymer, Middle Temple, London, February 18, 1771, Misc. Ms. Collection, APS.

[13]See, for instance, John Lord Campbell, *The Lives of the Chancellors and Keepers of the Great Seal of England from the Earliest Times Till the Reign of King George IV* (London, 1850), VI, 371.

[14]Robert Crafton to Bond, London, December 16, 1773, CAD COLL, PB, "Biog." Box.

[15]*Pennsylvania Gazette,* May 5, 1773.

[16]The sworn evidence of Phineas Bond, February 15, 1785, before the Commissioners for American Losses, PRO, AO 12/38.

[17]Cashbook of Phineas Bond for 1776, PRO, AO, 13/70A.

[18]Inventory of Dr. Phineas Bond's estate, August 29, 1774, administered by the Registrar of Wills, Mrs. Williamina Bond, and Phineas Bond, Esq., CAD COLL, PB, "Misc. Bond" Box.

[19]Indenture by Bond, June 3, 1773, Record of Deeds, County of Philadelphia, D34, 509.

[20]See Bond's evidence before the Commissioners of American Losses, PRO, AO 12/38.

[21]See Association Papers, May 1775, Peters' Mss., HSP, p. 45; the Clymer Mss., HSP, p. 5.

[22]See Commissioners of American Losses, PRO, AO 12/38.

[23]Minutes of the Supreme Executive Council of Pennsylvania, Sunday, August 31, 1777, *Colonial Records* (Harrisburg, 1852), XI, 283–284.

[24]Bond to President Wharton, Chestnut Street, September 3, 1777, *Pennsylvania Archives*, Samuel Hazard, ed. 1st Series (Philadelphia, 1853), V, 578–579.

[25]See Thomas Gilpin, *Exiles in Virginia: With Observations on the Conduct of the Society of Friends During the Revolutionary War, Comprising the Official Papers of the Government Relating to that Period, 1777–1778* (Philadelphia, 1848), pp. 65, 69.

[26]Gilpin, *Exiles,* pp. 92 ff.

[27]*Colonial Records,* XI, 290, 300.

[28]Gilpin, *Exiles,* p. 122.

[29]Sophia Logan Fisher, "A Diary of Trifling Occurrences: Philadelphia, 1776–1778," Nicholas Wainwright, ed. *Pennsylvania Magazine of History and Biography,* LXXXII (Philadelphia, 1958), 450.

[30]Joseph Reed, President of Pennsylvania, July 27, 1780, *Penna. Archives,* 4th Series, III, 774.

CHAPTER THREE

Exile

Early in November 1778, Bond arrived in London and immediately set about reinstating himself at Middle Temple. As soon as he was enrolled, he moved from the Portos in St. James Street to more modest lodgings at Mary Correge's boarding house where rooms and daily breakfast cost £5-18-3 a month. Bond had brought his library with him, carefully packed in thirty-six cases. By year's end, he was comfortably settled, busy filling calf-bound books with copious notes on legal cases and decisions and expecting shortly to win his degree.[1] Had it not been for his conscience, the war would have seemed a blessing in disguise.

But Bond could never forget that he had abandoned the ladies. Of course at first he believed the separation would be only "for a Time;" the British armies would soon be victorious; the rebels would be suppressed; Bond would be able to return to Philadelphia in triumph, as it were, and as a barrister able to provide more effectively for the family than in the past. There was the added consolation that his mother was no ordinary woman; she was a born manager with a head for business. Nothing appeared to give her more pleasure than speculating in western land, or buying and selling properties in Philadelphia, or going to court to collect debts, or in general proving herself successful in a man's world.[2] Also Bond never doubted that his cause was just.

Before he reached manhood, when he was weak and puny, unable to look after himself, His Britannic Majesty had protected him. It was a gift, freely given, that demanded repayment. He owed his sovereign natural allegiance and had done only what any full-blooded subject ought to have done under the circumstances. Even when the exile proved longer than Bond had anticipated, he was able to write that "my Attachments . . . have been long since fixed, and . . . have suffered no Diminution—or Alteration."[3]

Nonetheless, it was with enormous relief that in the winter of 1779 Bond learned of his sister Williamina's marriage to General John Cadwalader. As commanding officer of Philadelphia's first city troop, Cadwalader could offer the Bond ladies the protection they required. At once Bond wrote to his new brother-in-law that "it is no small Comfort to me to think that in You they have a friend."[4]

The good news marked the beginning of one of Bond's happiest years. In June, he received his call to the bar. At the end of the year, the treasury lords, impressed by the evidence of the Erskines and the Wemysses—distant relatives of Bond—granted him an annual pension of £100 sterling for losses sustained as an American Loyalist. Later the amount was doubled.[5] The allowance enabled Bond to leave Mary Correge's boarding house.

At the beginning of 1780, he moved to No. 5 Brick Court, in Middle Temple; built, it was said, in the eleventh year of Elizabeth's reign. For £25 sterling a year Bond had the rooms "2 pairs of stair high" on the west side of the staircase. Each evening Mrs. Samuel Birks came to light the lamps; William Buller called daily to clean the shoes; a valet took care of Bond's other needs. The barrister purchased a key to the Temple gardens. There on pleasant days he must have strolled and admired the famous sun dial.[6]

Furthermore, as the fees increased, Bond's wardrobe grew. He bought fluted-silver buckles for his shoes, a sword for state occasions, and quantities of waistcoats: there was a lemon, a pink, and a blue striped; several that were trimmed with gold braid; two cashmeres; and one white silk, one scarlet, and one black silk. He purchased lawn stocks by the dozen and beaver hats, two and three at a time. Each fall Bond made a point of spending at least a week at Frank Rogers in Margate for the bracing effects of the sea air.

In short, he lived like a gentleman. Although he must watch pence and shillings, "everything," he admitted, "is good or bad by Comparison—mine therefore is a most enviable Situation, compared to hundreds of my Countrymen, who from a State of Affluence, nay Luxury, are, with their helpless Families, reduced to extreme Indigence."[7] Finally, Bond was in England; that to him was the same as being in heaven.

But the war continued. The separation lengthened and Bond had been in exile "five tedious Years," as he worded it, when finally peace came. Then it was the wrong kind of peace. Instead of bringing joy, it seemed as though "the Door of Pity and Forgiveness" slammed shut in his face. There were Loyalists who left London for the United States. Bond bade farewell to William Rawle, to John De Normandie, to scores of others. But none of these friends had been attainted for high treason. Even without that stigma, once they were in America, Bond received letters from them describing the cold receptions which they had met. John de Normandie wrote he could not "urge any Man to return at least for the present."[8]

By the end of 1783, Bond faced the ugly possibility that he might never again be able to visit Philadelphia. He tried to break the news gently to his sister, Williamina Cadwalader. "Whatever may be my Lot," read Bond's letter to her, "I am conscious I can never be happy in a Separation from those I hold most dear on Earth:—but how long it may be advisable to continue that Separation:—or whether it can ever be overcome upon a footing of Security and a probability of Happiness must depend upon a vast Variety of Circumstances indeed."[9] He had been too subtle; letters continued to arrive from the family urging him to return. Bond was obliged in February of 1784 to make the following declaration:

> . . . as Things are now circumstanced, I know of no earthly Consideration that would tempt me to risque the irksome Situation to which Persons of my way of thinking are Subject; and, to which they must be subject, 'till a candid manly way of acting and judging succeeds to the narrow Prejudices which are but too prevalent —I do not speak out of Book, believe me; I have lately, even here seen some Specimens of Harshness and unrelenting Severity . . . I for the Present must unavoidably lay aside the Idea of visiting America . . . Let this frank unequivocal Declaration then content You.[10]

With the passing of each month his nostalgia heightened. In desperation he begged his sister Williamina to send her young son, Thomas Cadwalader, to London. Bond could offer him the finest education in the world and through the care he would lavish upon young Tom, "I could," he wrote Williamina, "show the love I bear for *You*." Even that hope died. Williamina's answer verged on the cruel. She refused because, explained her letter, never must her son "become disgusted with his own Country, after living and forming Connexions in *such a Heaven* as England."[11]

Each letter from home struck Bond as more heartrending than the last. At the end of 1783, he read that his grandfather, William Moore, had died. Six months later, he learned that his grandmother had followed the judge to the grave, and Moore Hall must be sold. The war had devastated it. First, Howe's army encamped on the farm, ruining the crops, breaking down the fences, commandeering grain and hay and horses and poultry and sheep, and decamping without leaving behind any receipts. Next, during the winter at Valley Forge, part of Washington's army quartered at the Hall. The family wanted four to five thousand guineas for the estate, but no one would offer a price; Pennsylvania was in a financial depression.[12] Bond must try and sell the plantation in England. Yet after the War for Independence Englishmen proved temporarily uninterested in property in the former colonies.

In 1785, Bond learned of the death of Williamina's youngest son, John. It became his lugubrious duty to order an English-made tombstone for the infant. Then the next year brought the harshest blow of all: General John Cadwalader was dead. Bond was agonized. "Everything I have heretofore suffered," he wrote, "falls short." This more than anything else increased "the heavy weight of Separation."[13]

Yet a shred of solace remained. Bond had caught sight of a way to end the long exile! There was a chance he might be able to return to Philadelphia in safety and with dignity.

Bond had won the trust and confidence of a powerful group of men: the merchants in the twenty-one "most considerable" London houses trading to the eastern and southern United States. To them Bond was the best possible barrister, "the Person," in their own words, "best qualified to advise them in the Security of their extensive Interests." He had "Integrity and Abilities . . ., respectable Connexions" in the middle states which abetted his efforts on their behalf, and was conversant with the commercial and local laws of both England and America.[14] Although many of Bond's clients thought well of him, it was the esteem and appreciation of this particular group of merchants that changed the course of his life, for by 1785 they were desperate men.

The war had been hard on them. It curtailed trade. Theoretically, of course, all Anglo-American commerce ceased. Actually, Bond's clients managed—at least for a time—to maintain a limited exchange. They established subsidiary firms in neutral European countries, especially in Holland and in the free ports of the West Indies. They set up houses in Amsterdam, Rotterdam, Curaçao, and St. Eustacia; changed their ships' registers and names so they might sail under the protection of neutral flags; brought Virginia and Maryland tobacco into London and sent British manufactures to the revolting colonies.[15]

No matter how ingenious, it remained an illicit and diminished commerce. The belligerent governments commandeered some of the merchantmen, captured others, and blockaded ports. Then, in 1780, Holland abandoned neutrality and entered the war against England.

The lack of business drove the small firms into bankruptcy.[16] Among them were a few of Bond's old accounts: Crafton & Colson, for instance, who had been one of the first to trumpet his praises, closed their doors in March 1778. For others the war simply lasted too long. William Neate died before peace arrived. Walter Ewer became ill in 1782 and went to Margate to recuperate. There he died on the 18th of October.[17]

The large companies survived, but they suffered. Some never regained their former prosperity. This was true, for example, of Bond's lifelong friend, Martin Petrie. Before the Revolution he had been the most powerful linen and calico merchant in London. The war so hurt his firm that Petrie was unable to rebuild it. Since he had four sons and five daughters to raise, he eventually abandoned trade and entered government.[18]

Still Bond's twenty-one houses would have weathered the war with greater ease had it not been for the American debts. They had extended such liberal credit terms to their colonial customers, that on the eve of the revolution Americans from South Carolina to

Massachusetts owed them money.[19] A single Maryland merchant company owed twelve of Bond's clients the enormous sum of £150,000 sterling. With the commencement of hostilities payments on both principal and interest stopped. State after state proclaimed moratoriums on all debts due British subjects contracted before 1775 or 1776. Virginia and Maryland went further and passed tender laws, which enabled their citizens to discharge debts to non-resident creditors by lodging depreciated currency in the state treasuries.[20]

The investments frozen in America plagued Bond's clients far more than the lack of trade. To protect those assets they helped establish "The Committee of London Merchants Engaged in the North American Trade" and through that organization kept parliamentarians and ministers apprised of the problem of the debts.[21] By 1782, when the war was drawing to a close, government had heard "the Voice of the British Merchants." It had become the conviction of the ministry that parliament would reject any peace treaty that failed to provide for payment of the debts. As one observer put it, the desires of the merchants carried more weight "in Parliament than the interest of America or the British Empire."[22] The result was article four in the preliminary peace treaty of November 1782 which read:

> It is agreed that the creditors on either side shall meet with no lawful impediment to the recovery of the full value in sterling money of all *bona fide* debts heretofore contracted.

The hopes of Bond's clients soared. They could soon start proceedings for the recovery of their investments. They might institute suits in American courts. It seemed to them as though the worst was over. Moreover, the outlook continued to brighten during the first months of 1783.

On February 4, Britain proclaimed an official cessation of hostilities in America. On March 3, William Pitt introduced in the house of commons, "A Bill for the Provisional Establishment and Regulation of Trade and Intercourse between the Subjects of Great Britain and those of the United States of North America." The provisions, designed to eliminate the economic grievances that had led to the war, were extremely generous. American ships and vessels were to be treated as though they were British and were to be admitted "to all of His Majesty's islands, colonies, and plantations in America." Bond's clients were pleased. They stood for liberal economic relations with the United States; otherwise their American customers might turn to the French or to the *entrepôts*.[23] Hoping Pitt's measure would lead to an Anglo-American commercial treaty, they gave it wholehearted support.

Meanwhile, the merchants claimed Bond's full attention. He must advise them on how to institute suits in the United States; he must hire agents and factors, draw up necessary powers of attorney, and write detailed instructions for the guidance of the representatives. Bond was so busy he missed opportunities to send letters to Philadelphia by personal conveyors. He was obliged to apologize to the family for his silence and to explain how he "was very much pressed for Time" and had at present "very little Leisure."[24]

As reports came in from the states, Bond's hopes for quickly settling the mercantile cases dissolved. At the end of 1783, he heard from the Virginia debtors, Ross, Pleasants & Hay, that they were "just emerging, as it were, from a State of Bankruptcy." They had lost a thousand hogsheads of tobacco to the state of Virginia in payment for notes passed by their senior partner when he was commercial agent in the late war. They doubted they would ever see the tobacco again, supposing it had sunk into the "general public debt for the payment of which no adequate provision will probably be made in our time." A few weeks later, they wrote again explaining that "the situation of the Company's Affairs hath been distressing beyond measure for some time past occasioned by . . . a great backwardness in our Customers to make payment." In March, they reported that the winter was severe, that blizzards and continued cold were keeping the rivers frozen over and the roads impassable. "In short," the letter concluded, "little or no business hath been done in Virginia for six weeks."[25] It became clear to Bond that Ross, Pleasants & Hay Co. were not about to pay their debts.

The situation worsened. During 1784, state after state contravened article four in the peace treaty. South Carolina led the way. On March 26th, the legislature passed a bill prohibiting creditors from initiating suits until January 1, 1785, and providing if the creditor won the suit for principal to be paid in four annual installments starting in 1786 excluding interest accrued during the war years. In October, Virginia outlawed wartime interest and ordered that debts be paid in seven annual installments. In December, Pennsylvania legislated for payment in three annual installments starting in 1785. New York prohibited the initiation of suits until 1786 and, along with Massachusetts, suspended payment of wartime interest. Only Maryland seemed lenient. Suits could be started on January 1, 1784, but there Bond's agents ran into "hidden Impediments." Maryland judges could disqualify attorneys or refuse them admission to the bar on suspicion they were "unsatisfactory" to the state government—and they did.[26]

News of the laws stunned Bond's clients. How incredible it was that Americans would contravene an international agreement! "It is believed," wrote one merchant, "that no instance has occurred in the history of mankind, where the private property of individuals has been withheld, after being secured and guaranteed by national treaties."[27]

Bond's merchants had no sympathy for the American debtors nor for the fact that they simply had to have time in order to pay. Bullion was leaving the country in large amounts. As one Massachusetts trader wrote, "we are now . . . almost drained of money." He believed "many years will necessarily elapse before those Debts can be paid." Virginians claimed their debt to the British merchants was ten times the amount of their circulating cash. It was impossible to pay at once.[28]

On the other hand, Bond's clients had already waited nine years for their money. The prospect of having to wait three, or four, or seven more years was more than they could bear. They pointed out that time was the most precious of commodities: time lost vouchers; time weakened testimonies; time carried away agents, factors, and attorneys; time created widows and orphans; time ruined creditors, reducing them "from independence and ease, to poverty and indigence;" time removed the support on which many depended for their old age.[29] Nevertheless, by the end of 1784 they faced reality: they must wait for their remittances.[30]

Fear of bankruptcy grew; events at home were equally discouraging. Pitt's bill was lost, talked to death in a great debate over the economic consequences of the Revolution. Before the war America accounted for one half of British shipping, but now those vessels belonged to an alien country and in time of crisis could not be pressed into His Majesty's service. Yet during emergencies the Royal Navy always counted on commissioning merchantmen and recruiting the men who sailed them. If the bill passed, encouraging as it would the shipping of the United States and abolishing the navigation acts which were responsible for British sea power, Americans would gradually possess themselves of the carrying trade; the British would lose their nursery for seamen; and the kingdom, declared William Eden, "would decline and languish during peace, and would be helpless and dependent during war."[31] Member after member rose to present dire predictions of things to come: British artisans would emigrate to the United States carrying with them industrial secrets . . . American manufacturing would develop and soon out-rival British production . . . the hat trade would be lost . . . the sugar trade would go . . . shipbuilding would become a forgotten art. Hysteria seized the Commons.

Beyond the walls of parliament the debate transformed itself into a pamphlet war that raged for over a year. The West Indian planters, some members of the merchant class, and the followers of the new and still small free trade school presented the case for liberal relations with the United States. But the mercantilists, led by Lord Sheffield, convinced the majority of their countrymen that the former colonies represented the most dangerous rival they had in the world. "This country," wrote Sheffield "has not found itself in a more interesting and critical situation than it is at present. It is now to be decided whether we are to be ruined by the independence of America, or not." In comparison the peace was "a trifling object." For the present decision involves "not merely the greatness, but even the very existence of our country."[32]

Instead of a liberal trade agreement, the King in Council was regulating Anglo-American commerce through illiberal orders that supported the navigation acts and prohibited the United States from trading with the British West Indies and the Maritime Provinces. Charles Jenkinson, an old-line imperialist and staunch supporter of Sheffield, was dominating the Committee of the Privy Council on Trade while the chief clerk, George Chalmers, was dedicating himself to weakening the United States whenever and wherever possible. Instead of a spirit of amiability and harmony, hatred and fear of America were spreading throughout the kingdom. The mood seemed to foreign observers more hostile than when the actual fighting had been going on. One reported that if the treasury had another "hundred millions to spend," the people would force the Ministry into a war with America.[33] The chance for an Anglo-American treaty of amity, commerce, and navigation vanished.

Bond's merchants became desperate. Anti-British sentiment was rife in the United States; anti-Americanism in Great Britain. Customers in America were failing to honor their ancient obligations; some seemed to have no desire to pay. Bond and his battery of attorneys were powerless to litigate in view of the state laws. The traders felt the walls closing in on them. By 1785 they were open to any suggestion from any source. When it came from "trusted Mr. Bond," they seized it.

NOTES

[1]See invoices, CAD COLL, PB, "Voucher" Box and Bond's notebooks at the Historical Society of Pennsylvania.

[2]While Bond was in exile, Mrs. Bond rented the Chestnut Street house and purchased the Union Street property (see Chap. I) which she sold at a profit in 1793 to Eduard Duant, Record of Deeds, D 17,646; D 41, 130–131. See also memorial of Adam Haas of Germantown, August 15, 1777 for debt owed Mrs. Williamina Bond in the amount of £500 and the memorial of Dr. Thomas Parke, November 22, 1799, transferring 31 tracts of land in Northumberland County, Pennsylvania, amounting to 12,759 acres, to Mrs. Williamina Bond in fee simple in payment of note due April 10, 1795, CAD COLL, PB, "Misc. Bond" Box.

[3]Bond to Mrs. John Cadwalader, England, 1783, CAD COLL, PB, "Biog" Box.

[4]Bond to General John Cadwalader, London, April 13, 1779, "Biog" Box.

[5]See Register of Admissions of the Honorable Society of the Middle Temple from the Fifteenth Century to the Year 1944, H. A. C. Sturgess, ed. (London, 1949), I, 372; for the Commissioners' decision see Bond to Lord North, Middle Temple, August 19, 1780, PRO, AO 13/70A.

[6]See invoices, CAD COLL, PB, "Voucher" Box.

[7]Bond to Mrs. John Cadwalader, Middle Temple, February 11, 1784, "Biog" Box.

[8]Dr. John De Normandie to Bond, Philadelphia, October 20, 1783, "F-G" Box.

[9]Bond to Mrs. John Cadwalader, Middle Temple, February 11, 1784, "Biog" Box.

[10]Bond to Mrs. John Cadwalader, Middle Temple, February 10, 1785, "Biog" Box.

[11]Bond to Mrs. John Cadwalader, Middle Temple, February 10, 1785 and May 2, 1785, "Biog" Box.

[12]Miers Fisher to Bond, Philadelphia, November 17, 1784, "Biog" Box.

[13]Bond to Mrs. John Cadwalader, Middle Temple, May 5, 1786, "Biog." Box.

[14]The twenty-one houses were: Fludyer, Maitland & Co.; Ludlum & Lavry; Eddowes, Petrie & Ellis; Thos. Wetherall & Sons; Dan Mildred & Co.; M. Joy & Co.; Blackburn, Shirley & Co.; Charles Jackson; Bird, Dolly & Co.; Pitchard & Thoms. Royds & Co.; Edward Dowling & Son; Champian & Dickason; E. Lawrence; Warder, Dearman & Co.; Oxley & Hancock; Fredk. Pigou, Jr.; Thos. Corvello; Lane, Sons & Fraser; Harrison, Ansley & Co.; Jones, Havard, Jones & Co.; Harris, Quicott & Havard Co. See their memorial to the Marquis of Carmarthen, London, September 10, 1785, PRO, FO 4/3 and Robert Barclay, William Havard, Martin Petrie, E. Lawrence, and John Maitland to the Marquis of Carmarthen, London, July 22, 1786, FO 4/4.

[15]An example is the case of Ross, Pleasants & Hay Co. through whom a half dozen of Bond's clients bought tobacco during the war and sold British manufactures in America. Ross, Pleasants & Hay managed the feat by establishing the Ezekiel Edwards & Co. in Amsterdam and the John McGeorge & Co. in Curaçao and St. Eustacia. They changed the registers of their vessels, the *Experiment* and *Richmond,* from American to Dutch and thereby got tobacco to Holland where Edwards, in accordance with his instructions, sold it for British manufactures. See Daniel Ross to Ezekiel Edwards, Petersburg, Va., May 6, 1780, CAD COLL, PB, "Ross" Box.

[16]In 1781, seventeen London merchant houses closed their doors; in 1782, twenty-five; in 1783, thirty-eight. The relationship of those failures to the total number of English merchant bankruptcies was 34% and 45% respectively. See the *Gentleman's Magazine and Historical Chronicle* (London, 1781), LI, 96, 244, 295–296, 396, 492, 596; LII (1782), 47, 96, 152, 208, 264, 408, 456, 553; LII (1783), 83, 275, 455, 543, 630–631, 719, 807, 1067.

[17]*Gentleman's Magazine,* XLVIII, 191; CAD COLL, PB, "E" and "Neate-Misc." Boxes.

[18]See the obituary of Martin Petrie in *Gentleman's Magazine,* LXXV, 294.

[19]The Virginia house, Ross, Pleasants & Hay Co., for instance, owed Jones, Havard & Jones Co., over £2,000 sterling and Pitchard & Royds Co., £3,000 sterling. The Anglo-American firm, Wallace, Muir & Johnson (Wallace & Muir were tobacco merchants in Annapolis; Josuah Johnson resided in London) owed Eddowes, Nash & Petrie £50,374 sterling and eleven other clients of Bond £99,963 sterling. See Martin Petrie to Bond, London, August 6, 1789, CAD COLL, Thomas Cadwalader section, "Legal-Bond" Box; William Havard to Bond, London, March 5, 1788, CAD COLL, PB, "Ross" Box.

[20]Economists and statesmen both in America and England questioned whether the credit terms had not been too generous. In 1784, Lord Sheffield, the British mercantilist, claimed the liberal credit system had made bankrupts of three-quarters of the London merchants trading to the United States. Thomas Jefferson, who himself on the eve of the Revolution owed £10,000, thought the credit system a diabolic machination by which the London merchants kept the

Virginia planters eternally in their debt and at their mercy. As early as May 1774 Jefferson and Patrick Henry offered a proposal in the Virginia Assembly that all payments on British debts should stop. See John Lord Sheffield, *Observations on the Commerce of the American States,* (2nd ed., Dublin, 1784), p. 201; Robert O. DeMond, *The Loyalists in North Carolina during the Revolution* (Durham, N.C., 1940), p. 25; Jefferson to M. de Meusnier, Paris, 1786, *The Writings of Thomas Jefferson,* Paul L. Ford, ed. (New York, 1894), IV, 155.

[21]Edmund C. Burnett, "Observations of London Merchants on American Trade, 1783," *American Historical Review* (Washington, D.C., July 1913), 771–772.

[22]John Adams to John Jay, Grosvenor Square, May 25, 1786, *The Works of John Adams* (Boston, 1853), VIII, 395.

[23]The merchants drew up a pamphlet-size memorial, entitled, "Observations on the Trade, which before the Late War Subsisted Between Great Britain and that Part of America now Comprizing the United States with Some Regulations as appear Proper to be Adopted for the Recovery & Retention of a Considerable Part of that Commerce." They sent one copy to Pitt and one to the king. See Burnett, "Observations of the London Merchants," *AHR,* July 1913, 776.

[24]Bond to Mrs. John Cadwalader, England, n.d., CAD COLL, PB, "Biog" Box.

[25]Thomas Pleasants, Jr. to Edwards, Raleigh, December 1, 1783; David Ross to Edwards, Arrowfield, December 27, 1783; Ross to Edwards, Philadelphia, March 1784, CAD COLL, PB. "Ross" Box.

[26]The most concise listing of state laws impeding the recovery of debts is in *Secret Journals of the Acts and Proceedings of Congress* (Boston, 1821), IV, 187–194.

[27]Patrick Colquhoun, *Case of the British Merchants who Traded to America Previous to the Late War* (London, 1787), p. 8.

[28]Stephen Higginson to John Adams, Boston, August 8, 1785, "The Letters of Stephen Higginson," J. Franklin Jameson, ed. *AHAAR,* 1896, I, 719–720; Jefferson to Alexander McCaul, London, April 19, 1786, Ford, ed., *Jefferson,* IV, 202.

[29]Colquhoun, *Case of the British Merchants,* p. 9.

[30]For instance, on September 1784 the Committee of Glasgow Merchants Interested in the North American Trade passed a resolution that they were "willing to take payment of their American debts by yearly installments upon proper security not exceeding four years. . . ." They so informed the Virginia legislature. See the Miscellaneous Legislative Petition, 1784, Virginia State Library, Richmond, Virginia, Folder / December 17, 1784.

[31]*The Parliamentary History of England,* T. C. Hansard, ed. (London, 1803), XXIII, 607.

[32]Sheffield, *Observations,* p. 217.

[33]Adams to Jay, Grosvenor Square, July 19, 1785, *Works,* VIII, 282.

CHAPTER FOUR

Obtaining
the Appointments

During the summer of 1785, Bond heard the talk that was going around London about Sir John Temple. According to the gossips, Temple was going to the United States as consul general and as Britain's first, official representative. The news interested Phineas. As he interpreted it, the appointment must mean government was about to establish a consular service in the United States and other consuls would soon be commissioned. Why should not he be one of them? Temple too was an American Loyalist. If he could go back protected by the office he held, so could Bond. The more he thought about it, the more he wanted the post. He had been in exile now for seven years and yearned to be again in Philadelphia with his family. Furthermore, he certainly could do more for his merchant clients in Pennsylvania as a consul than in London as a barrister. Bond presented the plan to them. The merchants grabbed it like drowning men.

Were Bond to go out as consul for the middle Atlantic and southern states, where they had their interests, he could function in a dual capacity: as consul and as their overall agent. He could manage and advise in all their "Commercial Concerns." At the same time as consul he could negotiate with American officials and work for the removal of "the Obstacles and Inconveniences" under which traders were "labouring." They envisioned Bond appearing before the state legislatures, "pointing out the Defects in the System of Laws" and offering "Amendments as may overcome the Obstacles."[1]

Bond's clients presented the suggestion to the Committee of London Merchants. Upon receiving that body's approval, they drew up a memorial for the benefit of Francis Osborne, the Marquis of Carmarthen (later the fifth duke of Leeds). Carmarthen was Pitt's original secretary of state for the foreign department. He joined the ministry on the 23rd of December 1783. Although he was never one of the workers of this world, he possessed a keen mind, enormous personal charm, and tended to be a political realist.

Before the declaration of independence he had taken the hard line with respect to America, voting for the coercion acts and against Lord North's propositions for conciliating the differences. After the war he was ready to extend full recognition and exchange ministers with the United States. He and Pitt discussed the matter. But by the summer of 1784, the mood in parliament rendered such an appointment impolitic. The prime minister and the secretary of state agreed to bide their time. Until the situation on both sides of the Atlantic became more settled, they would move with caution.

On September 10, 1785, Carmarthen received the merchants' memorial. It read as follows:

> Being inform'd that Government intend shortly to appoint some Gentlemen to reside in various Parts of the United States of North America for the purpose of protecting the Commercial Interests of this Nation, and feeling ourselves most materially interested in the Credit & Ability of the Person to be appointed to the middle Departments of the United States with which we are most immediately connected, we beg leave to recommend to the Patronage of your Lordship Mr. Phineas Bond, a Gentleman well & long known to us, who was settled previous to the War at Philadelphia & had very deservedly established a Reputation for Legal & Commercial Knowledge & whose Attachment to this Country was conspicuous in withdrawing Himself from America soon after the Declaration of Independence—Since Mr. Bond's residence in England he has been admitted to the Degree of a Barrister & very frequently consulted by several Merchants engaged in the American Trade as a Person most conversant with the Local Laws of that Country & whom they of course deem'd best qualified to advise them in the Security of their extensive Interests.

> We have that Reliance & Confidence in Mr. Bond that we are of the Opinion it will be a material Acquisition to the Government & a great security to the Commercial Interests of this Country, if he be appointed to reside there in a Station suited to his Character & Ability.

And we are the more confirm'd in this Opinion from his
respectable Family Connexions resident there, who must ever give
a Countenance—and Sanction to his Efforts in our Behalf—We
therefore warmly recommend Mr. Bond to your Lordship's Notice
& Patronage.[2]

Eleven days later a subcommittee of five merchants (Messrs.
Barclay, Maitland, Oxley, Lawrence, and Petrie) presented the
memorial in person to Lord Carmarthen. They explained the un-
derlying reasons for it and enlarged on Bond's qualifications.
Carmarthen listened politely . . . then dashed their hopes. He
blandly informed them the ministry entertained no plans for sending consuls, other than Temple, to the United States.

It took the merchants three months to recover from the blow:
three months of committee meetings, discussion, and discourses on
the blindness of the foreign department. What nonsense to expect
"any one Person" to protect British commerce over "such an Extent of Continent." Clearly, government had no appreciation of the
difficulties encountered in the Anglo-American trade. The merchants must educate. They must point out to the foreign department that "Forms of Proof to ascertain Brit: Debts & to secure
British Property depend upon Acts of Parliament which no longer
extend" to America. They must spell out the loopholes in the bankruptcy laws, explain that in many states laws enabled creditors to
issue attachments against the debts and property of their nonresi-
dent debts, so that a single foreign creditor "by an early application, may gain an Advantage over the mass of Creditors . . . gain
a Preference as to his own Debts—and thereby postpone nay perhaps totally exclude the general Body of Creditors—." They must
inform my Lord Carmarthen that British merchants "had no means
of obtaining Payment of a recent Debt in North America thro' the
Channel of the Courts of Law there, no Commercial Treaty being
yet settled." And they had best remind him that the state legislatures had "universally restricted the Recovery of Debts contracted
before the War." Finally, they must make it clear that their object
with respect to Mr. Bond "extended much further than the mere
Protection of Trade."[3]

A second memorial on behalf of Bond came into being. It

included each of the above points and ended with the ominous re-
mark that were trade not soon eased, the British wholesale dealers
and manufacturers would find themselves, like the merchants, in
financial distress. The foreign office received the petition on December 14, 1785. The timing was perfect.

Six days earlier John Adams, America's minister to Great
Britain, had delivered a memorial to Carmarthen, demanding that
the British immediately evacuate the northwest posts, those frontier
fortresses along the southern shores of the Great Lakes. The forts
controlled the fur trade and the hinterland which on second
thought the British realized they had been hasty in ceding to the
Americans. They were, therefore, reluctant to hand over the posts.[4]
Adams, on the other hand, was demanding evacuation whenever
Prime Minister Pitt and Secretary of State Carmarthen granted him
an audience. He always received the same answer: Great Britain
would transfer the posts when the United States lived up to article
four in the peace treaty. Still these were oral responses.

Because of Adams' memorial, Carmarthen must present Britain's position in writing, and that necessitated more than a mere
wave of the hand and an "Oh! to be sure! Nothing could be done
until the debts were paid." He was now obliged to quote chapter
and verse, present extracts from the laws of those states contraven-
ing the treaty, describe the merchants' experiences in trying to collect their debts, and perhaps enclose memorials from the various
merchant committees. And so when the merchants delivered their
second petition, Carmarthen was only too willing to talk with
them.

During the following weeks the Secretary of State conferred
with the London merchants and with Mr. Bond. From them he
gathered the information he required to answer Adams' memorial;[5]
in return he agreed there ought to be a commercial representative
in the United States and that person should be Phineas Bond.

Carmarthen liked Bond. In spite of the disparities in rank and
wealth the two had much in common. They were practically the
same age: Carmarthen was thirty-five; Bond, thirty-six. Both were
then single; both paid close attention to their dress and the cultivation of fine manners; both enjoyed the theater and worshipped
Mrs. Siddons; both were stubborn; and both had the affection and

respect of the people they served. The merchants were always true to Bond, and the foreign ambassadors in London were devoted to Carmarthen. When the Marquis resigned from office, for instance, the Dutch minister, Baron Nagel, broke down and wept.[6]

But, although Carmarthen readily accepted Bond as his protégé, that did not settle the appointment. There were long, drawn-out negotiations over the extent and style of the commission. It was finally decided that as consul Bond should cover the middle Atlantic states—New York, New Jersey, Pennsylvania, Delaware, and Maryland—and that the foreign office would send a third consul, George Miller, to take care of the southern states.

The "Style" of the commission presented a more serious problem. Carmarthen explained that consuls were not diplomatic agents. The principal duties of a consul were "to protect and promote the lawful trade and trading interests of Great Britain, by every fair and proper means" and to advise and assist "His Majesty's trading subjects, quieting their differences, promoting peace, harmony and good will . . . and conciliating, as much as possible, the subjects of the ₊two countries. . . ."[7] But, pointed out Carmarthen, when settling commercial differences the consul might deal only with local administrators. Should the "matter of complaint" necessitate settlement by higher authorities the consul would be unable to operate. In other words, it was Carmarthen's conviction that the United States government would never permit Mr. Bond to confer with state legislatures and officials. It was still fresh in the secretary's mind that when Sir John Temple had tried to negotiate with the United States Congress on behalf of the Loyalists, John Jay had sent a note to the British foreign office stating that "the office of Consul General does not extend to matters of this kind."[8] Afraid that foreign nations would, instead of ministers, send consuls and use them to deal directly with the states, ignoring the Continental Congress, American statesmen were carefully defining and limiting consular jurisdiction.[9]

As a solution, Carmarthen suggested Bond should have two commissions: he should go to America as consul and also as commissary for commercial affairs for all the United States. The latter was an ambiguous office, a point in its favor. One authority on international law defined commissaries as ministers of the second rank who did not directly represent their sovereign but were useful in carrying on "an Intrigue with Safety, where the Secret is more necessary than Pomp."[10] Governments occasionally employed commissaries, and commercial treaties provided for them. According to custom such officers had the authority to negotiate with both local and federal governments on all commercial matters.[11] The post, therefore, seemed made to order for Bond.

On February 3, 1786, the merchants submitted a third memorial expressing their "Desire that to the Appointment of Consul . . . might be annexed, a Power to act as Commercial Agent for the whole Continent."[12] That settled the extent and style of the commissions. But then Bond began to entertain doubts about the project.

Going to America meant abandoning the law practice he had been so painfully building for the past eight years and which was just beginning to prosper. It meant giving up his annual pension of £200 sterling and perhaps forfeiting whatever settlement the commissioners for American Loyalists might award him. Indeed, when the commissioners learned he had received a governmental post, they might consider that sufficient compensation and drop his case. Suddenly it seemed to Bond as though he was about to sacrifice himself for the benefit of the London merchants.[13]

Then, in a conversation toward the end of February, Under-Secretary Frazer let it drop that the foreign office had no plans to remunerate him; they assumed the Committee of London Merchants would take care of the financial end of the appointments. Bond was ready to throw up his hands. He knew the merchants never contemplated paying him a salary as consul or as commissary. They "took for granted . . . it was to be a public Expense."[14]

At once Bond reported the development to his friends. They were as surprised as he but promised to wait upon Carmarthen and have the matter straightened out to Bond's satisfaction. Nevertheless, Bond decided that whatever the result he was not crossing the Atlantic until he received every possible security regarding his personal finances.

On March 3rd, the usual merchant subcommittee interviewed the secretary of state and explained why they thought "a competent Salary should be a public Expense." Carmarthen acquiesced. He had tried to save the treasury money. Since the merchants objected, he turned around and offered Bond £700 sterling per annum.[15]

Still Bond hesitated. He told Carmarthen "he was unwilling to relinquish the Prospect, his professional Pursuits afforded him, of a competent Support in England, until it was settled and defined by his Majesty's Ministers that his Allowance . . ., as an American Loyalist, should be resumed as soon as the Salary annexed to his . . . Commissions terminated." The Marquis sympathized. He assured Bond he would take the matter up with the treasury lords and have them inform the board that Bond's pension was to revive the moment his appointments ceased. Carmarthen also promised to see that Bond got whatever general settlement the Commissioners on Loyalist Claims allotted him regardless of whether or not he was holding a governmental office. Bond could ask for no more.[16]

At the end of March, Bond knew he was going to America. Until then he had kept silent about his opportunities. He had not written a word to his family. Now, he informed his mother but begged her to consider the news as highly confidential. Bond had learned that in politics a candidate never really had an appointment until he held the commission in his own hands. By early April, he had the credentials. "I wish I could speak with Certainty of the Time of my Departure," he then wrote, "but I am in the Power of Great Men and must wait their Pleasure."[17]

He prepared for the trip. He bought presents for the family. He went to see Charles Dilly, the book dealer, who agreed to send him all parliamentary acts that pertained in any way to trade or to American affairs. Bond told the Erskines; and Thomas passed on the news to his brother, the Earl of Buchan, who thought it particularly grand Bond had been recommended to government "by the united Voice of our Merchants trading to America."[18]

Meanwhile the summer passed and Bond remained in London. He attended frequent conferences at Whitehall and worked closely with Frazer, the under-secretary of state. Together they hammered out a consular plan for the United States which organized the service according to districts. Once that was accomplished the foreign department was ready for Bond to begin his mission.

On the 4th of September, Carmarthen gave him a letter of introduction to Temple. On Wednesday, the 7th, Bond kissed the hand of His Britannic Majesty. On Thursday, he took formal leave of his patron, the Marquis of Carmarthen. Bond received his final instructions and then left London for Falmouth, the packet *Swallow,* and the long trip to America.

NOTES

[1]London merchants' memorial to Carmarthen, December 14, 1785, FO 4/3.

[2]London merchants' memorial to Carmarthen, September 10, 1785, FO 4/3.

[3]Memorial of December 14, 1785, FO 4/3.

[4]For an analysis of the relationship of the fur trade to the retention of the posts see Samuel F. Bemis, *Jay's Treaty, A Study of Commerce and Diplomacy* (New York, 1924) Chap. 1; for a study that weighs the Indian question as the chief motive behind Canadian reluctance to transfer the posts see A. L. Burt, *The United States, Great Britain, and British North America* (New Haven, 1941), pp. 82–96. Adams' memorial is in the *Secret Journals of the Acts and Proceedings of Congress* (Boston, 1821), IV, 156–157.

[5]See Carmarthen to Adams, St. James, February 28, 1786, *Secret Journals,* IV, 189.

[6]See Oscar Browning's introduction to *The Political Memoranda of Francis Fifth Duke of Leeds* (Westminister, 1884), pp. i–iv; see also pp. 168–169, 174 and the author's article, "The Marquess of Carmarthen and the United States, 1783–1791," *History Today,* XIII (London, February 1963), 108.

[7]See Robert Fynn, *British Consuls Abroad* (London, 1849), pp. 41–43.

[8]*Journals of the Continental Congress, 1774–1789,* Roscoe R. Hill, ed. (Washington, D.C., 1936), XXIX, 887; XXX, 4.

[9]The United States had refused, for instance, to conclude a consular convention, begun in 1781, with France, the great ally, because under the provisions French consuls would submit their commissions directly to the state governments, bypassing Congress, and thereby awarding sovereignty in foreign affairs to the states. See the Chev. de la Luzerne's Convention, Articles 1 and 2 in *Secret Journals,* III, 7; see the excellent study by Alexander DeConde, *Entangling Alliance: Politics and Diplomacy under George Washington* (Durham, N.C., 1958), pp. 22–24.

[10]Monsieur de Wicquefort, *The Embassador and his Functions,* Trans. John Digby (London, 1776), pp. 33, 41.

[11]See, for instance, Article 26 in the Prussian-American Treaty of Amity and Commerce, *Secret Journals,* IV, 41; and Article 21 of the American-United Netherlands consular convention, *Ibid.,* VIII, 504.

[12]See London merchants' memorial, July 22, 1786, FO 4/4.

[13]See affidavit by Bond, sworn before Edward Shippen, president of the county court of common pleas, Philadelphia, November 13, 1788, PRO, AO 13/70A.

[14]Merchants' memorial, March 3, 1786, FO 4/4.

[15]See Bond to Lord Grenville, private, St. Alban's Street, February 9, 1793, FO 5/2.

[16]See Bond to the Commissioners of American Claims, Middle Temple, September 4, 1786, AO 13/70A.

[17]Bond to Mrs. John Cadwalader, Middle Temple, April 12, 1786, CAD COLL, PB, "Biog" Box.

[18]Buchan to Franklin, Edinburgh, September 3, 1786, Letters to Dr. Franklin, APS, XXXIV, 139.

CHAPTER FIVE

Waiting to be
Recognized

Upon arrival in the United States Bond must, before doing anything else, wait upon the British consul general there, Sir John Temple. Diplomatic protocol as well as Carmarthen's final instructions made the call obligatory. But Bond dreaded it.

For an entire year Temple had enjoyed a unique position in America: he had been the sole, official, British representative. He had established himself as a leader of New York society, had made a custom of entertaining members of congress and of the foreign delegations, and of welcoming every important stranger who came to town. He had become friends with Jay, the American foreign secretary. The "first People" of the capital respected Tuesday evenings as belonging to Sir John and Lady Temple.

The advent of Bond would automatically alter Temple's situation. There would then be two British officials in the United States. Moreover, as commissary for commercial affairs Bond would outrank the consul general. That Sir John might find hard to accept.

To Temple, Bond would seem young and inexperienced. Sir John was in his midfifties and a man of affairs. Before the war he had been lieutenant governor of New Hampshire and had sat on the council boards of five other provinces. He had served in England as surveyor general of the customs. While Bond was fleeing Philadelphia in the wake of Howe's army, Temple was sailing up the Delaware on a secret mission for His Britannic Majesty. Although unsuccessful, he received £2000 sterling for his efforts and later was knighted.[1] Bond, on the other hand, as a struggling barrister had been delighted with a £200 pension.

Then too the commission naming Bond consul for the middle

Atlantic states included New York, the state where Temple resided and which he considered as his particular domain. That Bond was now to have it would, at the very least, annoy Sir John. It might even give rise to one of his notorious temper tantrums. He had already—as Bond had learned—fought one duel in which he had wounded his opponent. He would later go so far as to cane a United States senator.[2]

Bond knew that the foreign department had left Temple uninformed about the appointments. Not until the 6th of September, when Bond was on the verge of leaving England and was going around Whitehall bidding farewell to the foreign office personnel, had Carmarthen written to Temple, explaining the commissions. The note instructed Sir John to give Mr. Bond "all the Assistance in your Power in the accomplishment of the Business with which he is charged."[3] That letter and Bond crossed the Atlantic together on the same packet boat.

The vessel reached New York on Wednesday, the 15th of November 1786. Although Bond was anxious to accomplish his New York business and get to Philadelphia, he deliberately waited two days before calling on Temple to give time for the delivery of Carmarthen's instruction.

On Friday, the 17th of November, Bond entered the consul general's office. He presented his credentials. Temple waved them aside, saying he had already been informed by "my Lord Carmarthen." The delay had been worthwhile. Still Bond's fears about the interview were justified. Temple was angry. At once, he announced that "he entertained the gravest doubts" regarding the construction of Bond's commission.

"His Majesty's Commission," said Temple, "appointed me to be Consul General in the United States of America, to reside wherever Congress sit to do Business. Congress ever since my Arrival, have set at New York, where I have regularly done all the Business that was in the Power of a Consul to do."

What exactly, Temple wanted to know, was the meaning of Bond's appointment, which was "subsequent to mine?"[4]

Bond brought to bear all the tact at his command. He told Temple it was his understanding his appointments were not in the least to interfere with the consul general's, and that the only reason the foreign department had extended his commission to New York was "in Consequence of an Idea prevailing in England, that the Congress was about to establish federal Towns in two different Parts of the Continent as the occasional Residence of that Body."

In trying to placate Sir John, Bond resorted to ancient history. It was true that in 1783 Congress had resolved to establish two capitals, but in 1784 they rescinded the plan in favor of a single capital on the banks of the Delaware. Still, Congress was itinerant. They had convened in Annapolis, Baltimore, York, Lancaster, Philadelphia, Princeton, Trenton, and New York. Their wanderings over the countryside had given the wits material for countless jokes. Bond's point, therefore, had some relevance and he pursued it.

"As the Terms of the Commission of the Consul General," continued Bond, "confine his Residence to the Place where the Congress might assemble, it was deem'd improper to leave a State, of so much Importance as that of New York unprotected, if the Removal of Congress from thence should occasion the Consul General to change his Place of Residence:—that State was therefore included in the District I have the Honour to superintend."

"But," Bond hastened to add, "I consider it to have been the Sense of Government, that I should refrain from the Exercise of all Powers, as Consul, in that State, while his Majesty's Consul General remains there." That seemed to appease Temple; Bond further reassured him by explaining that he planned to live in Philadelphia and was eager to leave New York as soon as possible.

Nonetheless, Bond felt it necessary to clarify his position. He pointed out to Temple that as commissary for commercial affairs he might be obliged to come to New York to make representations to the legislature "in common with other individual States, thro' out the Continent of North America."[5]

Temple answered that he "need not say any Thing" about that commission. The worst of the interview was over. The conversation turned to other things.

The consul general warned Bond about distressed British seamen who would be appealing for help. The navy board, explained

Temple, wished to encourage the return of seamen; Bond could count on the British packets to carry them and on the naval allotment of six pence a day.[6]

Next, Temple questioned Bond about distressed British vessels. There was then a damaged one in New England. As usual government had left the consul uninformed about policy. Bond was delighted to be of assistance. He had brought with him a copy of the latest Act for the Increase and Encouragement of Shipping and Navigation.[7] In accordance with the act, answered Bond, a British vessel could not be repaired in a foreign port unless the damage was so extensive it precluded the continuance of her voyage. In that case and if the damages exceeded fifteen shillings a ton, the British consul must have "two fit and proper persons" survey the ship and submit a report which the consul must certify. Only then could the ship's master proceed with the repairs without endangering the vessel's right to be considered a British ship.[8]

Temple was properly grateful and Bond, anxious for the consul general to like him, went out of his way to be polite. He admired a ring Temple was wearing. Sir John was flattered. Although he could barely tolerate Bond, he never forgot about the ring. He made a notation in his will, leaving it to the consul at Philadelphia.[9] And so the interview ended on a pleasant note.

Good manners and tact had saved the day, but they had failed to change fundamental antagonisms. In December, Temple was as irritated over Bond's appointments as he had been in November. In a letter to Carmarthen he let the foreign office know exactly how he felt. He even tried to counteract Bond's influence by recommending one of his own friends for the consulship "in the Eastern district, upon a similar appointment with that of Mr. Bond for the middle district."[10] The maneuver failed. Whitehall's man in America was Bond not Temple. And Temple's rancor remained. The consul general never cooperated fully with the Philadelphia consul. Temple was always slow in replying to letters from Bond— sometimes he entirely failed to answer.

Meanwhile, Bond must make one other call before leaving New York. He must present his credentials to John Jay, the American secretary for foreign affairs. That proved to be a short visit.

Jay was polite, but he was noncommittal. He explained that congress was not then in session. As soon as it convened he would send the commissions to the legislative body for action.[11] Until then Jay could do nothing about the appointments.

Bond had completed his New York business. There was no further reason for him to stay in the city. On the 18th of November he left for Philadelphia for the house on Union Street and the joyous reunion with mother and sisters, and for a long period of comparative inactivity.

Until the continental congress recognized Bond's commissions, he was without official standing in the United States and unable to act on behalf of the London merchants or the British government. He had no authority to establish a consulate. As a result, Bond lived with his mother and waited impatiently for congress to convene.

He had a long wait. By the winter of 1786–1787 Congress was entering upon its last days. It lacked the respect of the people, funds, and congressmen. Day followed day without a sufficient number of members present to form a quorum. November passed without congress convening. December went by and there was no congress. By the first of January Bond had reached the conclusion that "in the present state of the federal Union; there is no saying . . . when a Congress will be formed."[12] And January's thirty-one days came and went without a session.

At the start of February, Bond wrote to Under-Secretary of State Frazer and confessed he was both embarrassed and "weary of repeating to the Marquis of Carmarthen the situation in which I still continue to stand: there has not been a congress assembled since I arrived, and when that body will meet again seems quite uncertain."[13] By then Bond was so disgusted with the inactivity of the federal government he doubted if it mattered very much whether congress convened or not, since "little efficacy can attend their deliberations." It was his conviction the states would be inattentive to any recommendations from congress concerning debts owed the British merchants and other infractions of the treaty of 1783. Bond saw America on the brink of a great constitutional crisis—as indeed it was. Before he arrived in the country the Annapolis Convention had met, and Alexander Hamilton had issued the invitation to the various states which was to result in the constitutional convention at Philadelphia during the spring of 1787.

During his first frustrating winter in America, Bond accomplished what work he could in an unofficial capacity. He talked with Philadelphia merchants and propagated information about the new British Act for the Increase of Navigation and Shipping. The reaction of the merchants amused him. They were perplexed and alarmed over the law, because if strictly enforced it would end the neat system they had devised of double papers and joint ownership of merchantmen. Bond described the deception for Carmarthen's benefit in the following words:

> . . . the practice of providing American ships with double Papers has been very successfully managed; and the Fraud had not only prevailed, to the Detriment of the Revenues in British ports but has even operated to elude those Duties which the Legislatures of the States have imposed upon British Bottoms: by an ingenious Collusion between Partners in Trade residing in different Countries, Ships have enjoyed the advantages of British Bottoms in Harbours within his Majesty's Dominions, and the Privileges of American Bottoms in the Ports of America.[14]

But according to the new act the only ships that could carry British papers were those built in a British port and owned by British citizens who—and here was the rub—were residents in Great Britain or in His Britannic Majesty's dominions. That, Bond was confident, would end the double-papers fraud.

He also prepared for the time when he could go to work for the London merchants. He wrote to friends and acquaintances in the different states asking them to send him "precise and accurate" details about laws that impeded the collection of debts owed the British. The moment congress recognized him as commissary for commercial affairs Bond wished to be in a position where he could immediately make representations to the various state legislatures. He reported these activities to Carmarthen and assured him that "I shall not dispense with my own Attendance even in the most remote States, where my personal Interference may be deem'd expedient to promote the commercial Interests of the Nation."[15] But the bad weather, impassable roads, and slow mails further frustrated Bond. The information he wanted trickled in at a snail's pace. The winter, he moaned, would be over before congress recognized him and he could apply to any of the state legislatures. By then they probably would have recessed. It was discouraging.

Although Bond worried about not being recognized, his unofficial status failed to stop stranded British citizens from searching him out. On the first of February, John Ewen came to Union Street. He was a British seaman, hungry, sick, and penniless, and he wanted to get back to England. If Bond could get Ewen to New York a British packet would carry him home. But the packets only sailed from New York City and the problem was how to get Ewen there. The man was too ill to walk, and the navy board's allowance of six pence a day would never cover the coach fare. Bond resolved the question by giving Ewen ten shillings from his own pocket. But he was only the first. By the middle of May Bond had spent £2-10- of his own money to man the British navy.[16] It was becoming an expensive project. Bond decided it was high time the foreign office was informed; he wrote, explained the problem and asked for a special allowance to take care of such situations.[17]

Meanwhile Bond's case came before congress. That body finally convened on the 2nd of February 1787. On the 3rd, they heard a report from the committee to whom Jay had sent Bond's commissions. On the 5th, congress decided to take no action on Mr. Bond but to refer the question back to Jay for his advice and recommendations.[18]

Since congress made a point of keeping secret its deliberations on foreign affairs, Bond knew very little about these events— which was probably just as well for his peace of mind. What he knew was that congress had at last formed and that his commissions were in the hands of a committee. As late as February 21st, it was Bond's understanding that the committee had not yet reported.[19] February passed and Bond heard nothing further.

In March his nervousness increased. He began to worry whether the attainder for treason might preclude his congressional recognition. An unpleasant incident occurred which made him uncomfortably aware that despite all the efforts of family and friends the attainder remained on the books.

As soon as Mrs. Bond had learned about the appointments, she had gone to see Charles Biddle, an old friend of Phineas and also vice-president of the Supreme Executive Council of Pennsylvania. She implored Biddle to quash the attainder. Since he was the kind of man who prided himself on keeping faith with friends, he agreed. On the 18th of April 1786, Biddle presented a petition to the executive council asking for the pardon of Phineas Bond. His eloquence persuaded a reluctant Council to suspend the attainder until the end of the next session of the general assembly.[20] But Council refused to do more, and a year later it became clear the attainder remained in force.

On the 29th of March 1787, the Pennsylvania comptroller general presented a report to the executive council asking that a debt in the amount of £233-17-8 due Phineas Bond, Esq. from Jacob Weiss be "forfeited to this Commonwealth by his attainder of high treason." Council approved the request.[21] Bond's anxiety heightened. What if the news of the forfeiture reached New York? Might it not adversely affect his chances for congressional recognition?

As it happened, the die was cast. Later Bond could look back on Thursday, the 29th of March 1787, as a critical date in his life—the day on which two American executive bodies deliberated his fate. In Philadelphia the executive council approved the comptroller general's report; in New York the Continental Congress heard Jay's recommendations concerning Bond's commissions.

Jay's letter was a thoughtful document which evaluated the recognition of Bond against the background of Anglo-American relations. The American secretary pitted the British infractions of the peace treaty against the American ones: Britain's retention of the northwest posts against the state laws impeding collection of debts due British merchants. Jay told congress "he would not be candid were he not to confess that in his Opinion Britain has more Reason to complain to the United States than the United States to Britain since the Peace. . . ." That was a point in favor of recognizing Bond; as Jay wrote, "it is in the Interest of this Country to be on good Terms with Britain."[22]

But, continued Jay's report, "his Britannic Majesty has no

treaty of Commerce with the United States, the admission of his Consuls and Commissaries by them, is a Matter of Favor and not of Right." The question then was whether the favor be extended?

One objection, as Jay saw it, was that the admission of Bond would "add to the Number of official Foreigners in this Country, who considering the Present State of our Commerce serve too much to watch and to circumscribe it." A second objection was that "according to the true sense and construction of" the commercial treaties America had made with France, Holland, Sweden, and Prussia, "The United States are not bound to receive any Consuls or Commissaries until after their Powers have been ascertained by Agreement."

On the other hand, reasoned Jay, the United States had received Sir John Temple in the absence of a treaty and had thereby set a precedent. To reject Bond, having accepted Temple, would add to the "asperities" already existent between Britain and America without achieving any positive result. Therefore, Jay recommended that "Phineas Bond, Esq. be . . . received and recognized as the Consul for his brit. Majesty throughout the States of New York, New Jersey, Pennsylvania, Delaware, and Maryland."

In treating Bond's other commission Jay was more outspoken. He argued that America had not received a single commissary for commercial affairs, that it was an ambiguous office, "that Commissions of this kind are not usual. That the precise Limites of the Authority conferred by it are not easy to ascertain;" and that it might function along ministerial lines. "The Power it gives him," Jay wrote, "is a Power that seems to place him in the Capacity of a Minister." It was uppermost in Jay's mind that Britain had not only failed to sign a commercial treaty but also to send a minister to the United States. He was determined Great Britain should not use Commissary Bond in place of a minister plenipotentiary. "Your Secretary," Jay told congress, "suspects that this Appointment was made to supply in some Sort the place of a Minister; and in his Opinion it will be most prudent not to let it take Effect." Those words destroyed Bond's chance for ever becoming commissary for commercial affairs in the United States of America.

On the following day congress debated the report.[23] There

was no question about the commissary appointment. Congress was only too pleased to follow Jay's suggestion and reject it. The debate revolved around the consular commission.

James Madison spoke first. He agreed with the secretary for foreign affairs regarding the violations of the peace treaty. Madison, too, considered America more in the wrong than Great Britain. But he disagreed with Jay that rejection of Bond would fail to produce concrete results. On the contrary, Madison suggested that Bond's rejection might produce a disposition in Britain to conclude a commercial treaty with the United States.

He also found it impossible to ignore, in his own words, "the indignity of Great Britain in neglecting to send a public minister to the United States notwithstanding the lapse of time since Mr. Adams' arrival there." Such "indignity," Madison pointed out, gave Britain "no titles to favor," while American self-respect demanded that Congress "should at least proceed with distrust & reserve" and reject Mr. Bond.

William Grayson followed, an outstanding orator and, on that day, Bond's strongest supporter. He appealed to congress' sense of propriety and argued "it would be good policy to admit Mr. Bond, and that it could not be decently & without offence refused after the admission of Mr. Temple."

The final and most vicious speaker was James Mitchell Varnum from Rhode Island. With flushed cheeks and loud oratory he "animadverted." He claimed a factor existed that the foreign secretary and the other delegates had ignored—it was the "obnoxious character of Mr. Bond." Varnum described in detail Bond's loyalist activities and attainder for high treason. They alone, he thought, were "sufficient reason for not admitting him."

It was then moved to postpone the question. All delegates voted "aye" with the exception of William Grayson. Bond's commissions were shelved.

That was April. Bond still had heard nothing about his appointments. He had written to Jay several times without receiving any satisfaction and finally concluded he must undertake the tedious journey to New York and wait in person upon the secretary for foreign affairs.[24]

At the end of April Bond was in New York and saw Jay. The Secretary promised to resubmit the commissions to congress; and on the first of May he did. Jay informed congress Mr. Bond had repeatedly applied about his appointments and begged congress to recognize Bond as consul, for after all it was "in *itself* not very important to either Country."[25]

On May 3rd, congress accepted Bond as consul for New York, New Jersey, Pennsylvania, Delaware, and Maryland, and rejected him as commissary for commercial affairs.[26]

Bond was still in New York. When he learned about the congressional action, he immediately called on Jay. The consular commission meant little to Bond. He and the British merchants had fixed their hopes to the commissary appointment. Bond argued with Jay. He explained about the merchants, assuring Jay that the appointment originated not with government, but with "a great body of the merchants of London." Jay remained unimpressed and rather unpleasantly informed Bond that in the absence of an Anglo-American commercial treaty he was fortunate congress had recognized even one of his commissions.[27]

Depressed, Bond returned to Philadelphia. He reported the events in a dispatch to Carmarthen. The situation, he thought, looked hopeless. "The suspension . . . of this Commission, my Lord," Bond wrote, "puts by, for the Present, the Exertion of the only Means from whence effectual Relief [for the British merchants] could result."

But Bond was due for yet another disappointment. Congress notified Pennsylvania about the consular appointment,[28] but before they got round to notifying the other states, they recessed because of their usual predicament—the lack of a quorum.[29]

On May 21, 1787, Pennsylvania recognized Bond as British consul,[30] but, as Bond must inform the foreign office, my "Commission has not yet been adopted by the other Four States, to which it extends." He felt like a pair of scissors with a single blade. He could only function in Pennsylvania and there only as consul. From his experience in America he concluded "it would be inexpedient to continue the Appointment of Consuls for Districts;—" and suggested that Whitehall employ agents instead. As convenient as it was for him to be in Philadelphia "for a few years," he candidly told Carmarthen, ". . . I should be loth to enjoy an expensive appointment unless I saw a prospect of rendering beneficial Assistance to Government."[31] In June 1787 he could see no such prospects.

July passed, and although congress reconvened they failed to notify the other states about Bond. He wrote to the foreign office that "The Proceedings of all public Officers on this Continent are so languid, it is most probable I shall have to make another Application to the Secretary for Foreign Affairs, to obtain a complete Recognition of that Commission. . . ."[32] The first of August found Bond again in New York.

This time he resolved to stay until he knew congress had notified New York, New Jersey, Delaware, and Maryland. August passed; it was not until the beginning of September that Jay finally informed Bond that "the Resolution of Congress adopting my Commission as his Majesty's Consul, is now transmitted to all the five States."[33]

After nine, long months Bond was able to start work as His Britannic Majesty's consul for the middle Atlantic states.

NOTES

[1]Temple was born in Boston in 1732; he died in New York City on November 17, 1798. The best biographical sketch is by Lewis Einstein, "Sir John Temple," *Divided Loyalties, Americans in England During the War of Independence* (London, 1933), Chap. 3; see also Rufus Wilmot Griswold, *The Republican Court or American Society in the Days of Washington* (New York, 1856), pp. 94, 95, 97; "The Bowdoin and Temple Papers," *Collections of the Massachusetts Historical Society,* 7th Series (Boston, 1907), VI, 80–105.

[2]See Esmond Wright, "Robert Liston: Second British Minister to the United States," *History Today XI* (London, February 1961), 123. The senator was John Rutherford.

[3]PRO, FO 4/4.

[4]Temple to Carmarthen, New York, December 7, 1786, FO 4/4.

[5]Bond to Carmarthen, Philadelphia, November 26, 1786, FO 4/4.

[6]Bond to Carmarthen, Philadelphia, May 15, 1787, *AHAAR,* 1896, I, 531.

[7]Bond wrote to Under-Secretary of State William Frazer on February 4, 1787, explaining he had brought a copy of the act with him "and found it particularly useful, immediately upon my Landing, in directing the Mode of Proceeding in the Repairs of a British Ship, then in some part of New England, about which the Consul General had been applied to: as he was not in possession of the Act, he was at a Loss what to direct, and I was happy in the Opportunity of communicating my Sentiments upon the Subject. . . ." *AHAAR,* 1896, I, 519.

[8]26 George III c. 60.

[9]Miss Rebecca Bond to Mrs. John Cadwalader, London, August 1811, CAD COLL, Thomas Cadwalader Section, "Rebecca Bond" Box.

[10]Temple to Carmarthen, New York, December 7, 1786, FO 4/4.

[11]Bond to Carmarthen, Philadelphia, November 26, 1786, FO 4/4.

[12]Bond to Carmarthen, Philadelphia, January 1787, *AHAAR*, 1896, I, 517.

[13]Bond to Frazer, Philadelphia, February 4, 1787, *AHAAR*, 1896, I, 519.

[14]Bond to Carmarthen, Philadelphia, February 21, 1787, *AHAAR*, 1896, I, 524.

[15]Bond to Carmarthen, Philadelphia, February 21, 1787, *AHAAR*, 1896, I, 522.

[16]Bill of Particular Expenses, Philadelphia, January 2, 1807, CAD COLL, PB, "Voucher" Box:

    1 February 1787 Gave John Ewen, Br. Seaman   £–10–
    7 March 1787 Gave James Jones, Br. Seaman   –5–
    15 May 1787 Gave Robert Micklejohn & 2 others   1–1–

[17]Bond to Carmarthen, Philadelphia, May 15, 1787, *AHAAR*, 1896, I, 531–532.

[18]*Journals of the Continental Congress 1787*, XXXII, 25, 29.

[19]Bond to Carmarthen, Philadelphia, February 21, 1787, *AHAAR*, 1896, I, 521.

[20]Charles Biddle, *Autobiography of Charles Biddle, Vice-President of the Supreme Executive Council of Pennsylvania, 1745–1821* (Philadelphia, 1883), p. 211; Minutes of the Supreme Executive Council of Pennsylvania, Tuesday, April 18, 1786, *Colonial Records*, XV, 8.

[21]*Colonial Records*, XV, 187.

[22]See *Journals of the Continental Congress 1787*, XXXII, 142–143.

[23]*Journals of the Continental Congress 1787*, XXXIII, 132 ff.

[24]Bond to Carmarthen, New York, May 1, 1787, *AHAAR*, 1896, I, 528.

[25]Jay to President of Congress, Office of Foreign Affairs, May 1, 1787, *Journals of the Continental Congress 1787*, XXXII, 249.

[26]*Journals of the Continental Congress 1787*, XXXII, 254, *Secret Journals*, IV, 243–244.

[27]Bond to Carmarthen, Philadelphia, May 16, 1787, *AHAAR*, 1896, I, 532–533.

[28]Charles Thompson, Secretary of the United States Congress to President Franklin, New York, May 4, 1787, *Pennsylvania Archives*, XI, 145.

[29]Congress lacked a quorum from May 11, 1787 until July 6, 1787.

[30]On Friday, May 18, 1787, the Supreme Executive Council of Pennsylvania met at Franklin's house. Thompson's letter declaring Bond consul was read "and an order taken that public announciation of him in that quality be made." *Colonial Records*, XV, 215. On May 21, 1787, President Franklin issued the formal proclamation: "Phineas Bond, Esq. having been recognized by the United States in Congress assembled, as Consul of his Britannic Majesty . . . It is hereby declared that all the Privileges, Preeminences and Authority which the Laws of Nations, and of the Land give to a Consul received by the United States, from any Nation, with whom they have no *commercial Treaty or Convention,* are due to, and shall be enjoyed, by the said Phineas Bond in this Commonwealth." Enclosure Bond to Carmarthen, Philadelphia, June 2, 1788, FO 4/6.

[31]Bond to Carmarthen, Philadelphia, June 3, 1787, *AHAAR*, 1896, I, 536.

[32]Bond to Carmarthen, Philadelphia, July 2, 1787, *AHAAR*, 1896, I, 538.

[33]Bond to Carmarthen, New York, September 2, 1787, *AHAAR*, 1896, I, 544–545.

CHAPTER SIX

Working Without
Instructions

Bond opened the first British consulate in Philadelphia during the autumn of 1787, after the Continental Congress had fully recognized him as consul for all the middle Atlantic states. Since he had no special funds and must draw upon his salary, he might have set up a very modest establishment. But Bond always tended to exaggerate his own importance and was ever serious about himself. The attitude accounted in large measure for the strengths and weaknesses in his character.

Determined to excel, he devoted himself to duty, worked tirelessly, and was perfectly willing to tackle problems that technically lay beyond the confines of his post. Such attributes set him apart from other consuls and for a time brought him the high esteem and respect of the home authorities. But concern with self, like a double-edged sword, cut in two directions. On the other side of the blade it made for prejudices. The boy, who had been instinctively drawn to the finer things in life, as a man emulated those with titles and wealth and assured social position; supported class distinctions; and looked down upon the great mass of people as inferior beings. He was unable to appreciate democracy and in his heart of hearts was afraid of it. Throughout his tour Bond remained fundamentally out of sympathy with American goals and ideals.

He arrived with his political convictions already frozen. In England he had closely followed the debate over the economic consequences of the war, accepting the imperialist point of view to the degree of practically memorizing the arguments of Eden, Sheffield, Jenkinson, and company. As long as their position dominated British policy, Bond's ideas mirrored those of the government. With the passing of the years changes occurred. His failure to alter basic convictions lessened his usefulness to the foreign department and eventually helped to carry him out of the main-stream of political activity.

But in 1787 he had a firm grip on the thinking of his superi-ors. As the only commissioned British official in Pennsylvania, he viewed himself as their eyes and ears, obliged to assume functions that ordinarily would be performed by "an Officer of higher dignity."[1] As a result the offices Bond opened resembled an em-bassy more than a consulate.

He took a house on the west side of Second Street near Chest-nut.[2] On the first floor were waiting rooms for those calling on business and the office where Bond held interviews and wrote his dispatches, sitting behind a desk that years later at auction brought the comparatively high sum of £42 sterling.[3] Beyond and on the upper floors were the living quarters, comfortably furnished for the consul and his guests. There were over a hundred chairs in the house, exclusive of benches, settees, and sofas. There were five servants: a cook, a valet, two maidservants, and a coachman.

The food at the consulate was good; the table handsome. Bond valued his silver at twelve hundred dollars; he bought sets of fine chinaware, together with platters, fruit and cake baskets, doz-ens of tumblers, goblets, brandies, and champagnes. He owned three dozen clarets, two dozen "lemonaders," and seventeen de-canters. The lamb and legs of mutton came from Butcher Smith; the "quartens," legs, and necks of beef, the veal cutlets, and tongues from Butcher Moore. Occasionally M. Marinot, the French caterer, sent in a supper of soup, *bouillie,* a kind of hasty pudding, two or three oyster pies, and *fricandeaux* of veal cooked in white wine. Bond imported his cheese from London and sent to Jamaica for casks of sugar and coffee and hogsheads of molasses. He kept his cellar stocked with twelve hundred dollars' worth of wines; bought Madeira by the pipe, porter by the cask, claret and port four to six dozen bottles at a time.[4]

After supper there might be card playing, or, if Bond had a single, congenial companion, a game of chess. Sometimes, when alone, he studied Swiss on chess and played out a game or two by himself; many evenings he read in his library. On the shelves were Samuel Johnson's *Lives of the Poets* in fifty-eight volumes and a ten-volume set of Shakespeare. There were geographies, histories, and political tracts; works by Adam Smith, James Pettit Anderson, Charles Fox, and Edmund Burke. There were translations of Voltaire and Necker, and bound volumes of the *Gentleman's Magazine,* which Charles Dilly, the London book dealer, faithfully sent Bond each month.[5] At night, the consul went upstairs alone to sleep in a great bed, with the curtains drawn around it, and under a quilt that came from Marseilles.

He continued to pay close attention to his wardrobe, which he insured for a thousand dollars. And when he moved into the consulate he bought a "chariot." Daniel Fraser gave it three fresh coats of paint and repaired two of the wheels, and Bond put his London friend William Havard to enormous trouble trying to procure a "front glass" for what Havard teasingly called, "his Excellency's Carriage."[6] At first two ponies pulled the vehicle, but Bond exchanged them for a more elegant pair of matching bays.[7]

On a salary of £700 per annum, he could barely afford this standard of living. Yet he was convinced the "enormous Expenses" were absolutely indispensable. Perhaps he was right; if he had not appeared so affluent, Philadelphia society might not have accepted him as graciously as they did and within a year called him "a great man."[8]

As it was, in his "chariot" behind George Story, the liveried coachman, Bond called on the Shippens and the Allens, the Drinkers and the Chews, the Clymers and the Penns. He attended tea parties and musicals at their homes together with eminent citizens like the Binghams, the Morrises, the Rutledges, Corbins, Harrisons, and Coxes.[9] In spite of Bond's past, the society into which he had been born received him, as one observer wrote, with the "respect and affection due to his acknowledged worth." This Bond found most gratifying.

While establishing himself socially, he was, at the same time, performing the principal duties of a consul: doing his utmost "to protect and promote the lawful trade and trading interests of Great Britain, by every fair and proper means . . .," and giving his "best advice, when called upon, to His Majesty's subjects."[10] Unlike some British and most American consuls of the time, Bond considered the post a full-time job.[11] He worked hard and made his official presence felt in the city.

Within six months, merchants, manufacturers, and members of the Pennsylvania government knew there was a British consul operating in Philadelphia. Bond had managed, within that short time, to curtail certain activities and stir up a "considerable Murmur" against himself, largely because he kept himself so well informed about what was going on.

He made a point of studying the local newspapers, especially the *Pennsylvania Herald,* the *Pennsylvania Gazette,* and the *Packet and Daily Advertiser.* He cultivated certain customs house officials who supplied him with the statistics and permitted him to see copies of manifests and bills of lading. Regularly Bond strolled along Water Street noticing what ships were in port, what flags they flew, what cargoes they carried, from whence they came and to where they were going. Periodically he went past the dry docks and checked the progress of ships being built. He lingered in taverns popular with traders to pick up odd bits of information. He kept close track of crop conditions, the state of the market, the amount of foreign orders, and the fluctuating exchange rate. He corresponded with acquaintances in other American cities. He called on merchant friends in Philadelphia and encouraged them to talk about their problems, their investments, and their plans for the future. And he listened to those who came to his office, not merely because many were distressed nationals and it was his duty to aid them, but because he could learn from the stories they told. Such, for instance, was the case of the two Englishmen, Edemsor and Royle.

Thomas Edemsor, a cotton merchant from Manchester, and Henry Royle, a calico printer from Chadkirk in Cheshire County, England, came to the British consulate during the second week of November 1787. Both were frightened; they were convinced their lives were in danger and if they remained in Philadelphia they would be assaulted, possibly killed. They told Bond a fantastic story.[12]

It began, according to Royle, in 1783, when an Englishman named Benjamin H. Phillips determined to start cotton manufacturing in America. In spite of all the parliamentary laws prohibiting the exportation of textile machines and the emigration of skilled artisans, Phillips went ahead with his plan. He sent his son to Philadelphia; then he bought a carding machine and three cotton spinners,[13] packed them in Queen's Ware casks, labeled them Queen's Ware, and had them loaded on the ship *Liberty*. Disguised as Wedgewood china, the machines passed customs. The *Liberty* sailed from Liverpool for Philadelphia with Phillips and the "Queen's Ware" safely on board. But before crossing the Atlantic the ship put in at Cork for additional cargo, and while there Phillips became too ill to continue the voyage. He returned to Liverpool where he died shortly afterward. Nonetheless the "Queen's Ware" sailed on and arrived in Philadelphia in the autumn of 1783.

Young Phillips claimed the casks. But without his father he was unable to use the machines; he sold them to another Englishman living in Philadelphia, Joseph Hague. Hague and some friends, according to Royle, "sat the said carding Machine and the forty-four thread spinning Machine to work." Fortunately, none of them knew how to operate the machines properly, and Hague lacked capital. He became "very apprehensive of the Expense," Royle said, "and soon discontinued the Use of the Machines and laid them by for some Time;" in the Spring of 1787, Royle bought them for sixty pounds Pennsylvania currency and then turned around and sold all four machines to Edemsor. He purchased them, claimed Edemsor, in order "to check the Advancement of the Cotton Manufactory in America." As a good Englishman ought, he "cut up" the machines—without injuring them—packed them in two cases, and in the middle of May sent them back to Liverpool on the ship *Grange*.

This was the act that had imperiled their lives. For shortly after the *Grange* sailed, certain Philadelphians, concerned over the state of the nation's economy, came together and formed "The Pennsylvania Society for the Encouragement of Manufactures and the Useful Arts."[14] They wanted to win economic independence from Great Britain by industrializing America; and as a first step resolved to establish cotton manufacturing in Philadelphia. They instituted a search for the machines Joseph Hague once owned and traced them to Royle and Edemsor. When they learned the spinners had left the country, the disappointment of some of the members turned to rage. They so very severely threatened the two Englishmen that Edemsor and Royle were "in great Dread of suffering from their Resentment."

For weeks Edemsor and Royle had been in hiding, waiting for the Society to lose interest in them, but instead of improving the situation seemed to deteriorate. "In the past few Days" the Manufacturing Society petitioned the Pennsylvania assembly for a law "to prevent sending Models abroad, and the seducing Artists and Manufacturers to quit the Country." Royle was a calico printer. If the law passed, he would be trapped in a state where he "was now looked upon," as he put it, "by so jealous an Eye of the People." He thought it "expedient" to leave at once. But he must have the consul's help; he lacked money for the passage home!

The story shocked Bond. Nothing he had previously heard or read about "American Seduction of British Machines and Artisans" had prepared him for the kind of zeal and fanaticism Edemsor and Royle described. He had no idea Americans were exerting such a determined effort to procure "the industrial secrets of the Old World," and that to achieve their ends they would stoop to violence.

Obviously, Bond was inclined to believe the two men. But a lifetime as a lawyer had bred caution. He must first check the facts. Bond brought the interview to a close, assuring Edemsor and Royle they would hear from him in the near future. As soon as they were gone, he began an investigation.

He tried first to locate Joseph Hague, only to find that that questionable character was no longer in the city. Rumor had it Hague was in England trying to procure machines and workers for the future cotton mills of Philadelphia. At once Bond passed this information on to the foreign office with the suggestion British officials might lay their hands on Hague "at a Place called Simmonthly, near Hayfield in Derbyshire."[15] Either Bond was too late or Hague too slippery. By March 1788, the rumors proved only too true: Hague had smuggled a carding machine into Pennsylvania! The legislature awarded him one hundred pounds for the machine, and the Manufacturing Society publicized the achievement in the press and urged "the propriety of gentlemen in every town . . . joining to procure one of 'the machines,' as they are of the greatest consequence to this country. . . ."[16]

Bond also learned that the bill the two Englishmen described to prevent "artisans" from leaving Pennsylvania was indeed being rushed through the legislature. It became his conviction that "The Society," in his own words, "instituted here for the Encouragement of Manufacturers . . . are very anxious to detain every Artist in the Country, whose Skill may have a Tendency to promote the Purposes of the Institution."[17]

In fact, Bond found the Society even more active than Edemsor and Royle had indicated. The organization was offering premiums for all kinds of industrial commodities and machines and, at the same time, was waging a full-scale publicity campaign for the purpose of inciting Americans in all states to establish manufacturing. Newspaper articles linked the scarcity of money in the United States to the scarcity of manufactures and attacked the "oeconomic maxim" that *we can buy goods cheaper than we can make them.* The Society advertised the benefits Great Britain had gained from industry; how the population in Manchester doubled during the past thirty years as a result of the cotton mills and how the same could be true for Philadelphia, Boston, or New York. Landlords were urged to employ capital in establishing "manufactories" which would attract workers to the cities and render empty houses and unimproved lots productive. To whet the appetites of profit-minded Americans, one article emphasized that, in the past year, the 143 British cotton mills with their 20,500 jennies had yielded "the immense profit to laborers and owners of the mills and factories, of £5,270,000 sterling." Another article called on "the planters of Maryland, Virginia, the Carolinas and Georgia . . . to pay the most immediate and the most *unremitted* attention to the cultivation of COTTON," so that the "middle and eastern states may become a Great Britain, with respect to arts and manufactures of all kinds. . . ." Now that Bond was interested in American manufacturing, it seemed as though every other issue of the *Pennsylvania Gazette* carried an editorial on the subject.[18]

From his investigations Bond reached three conclusions: first, that notwithstanding the Manufacturing Society's efforts American industries could not be quickly brought "to a State of Rivalship with those of Great Britain;" because, as he quite rightly pointed out, Americans were "essentially deficient in those main Sinews of Advancement: Money, fit Artificers, and fit Utensils."[19] "But," added Bond, and to him it was an important *but,* "when Matters of this Sort are in Agitation, it is fit to guard against an Evil, which tho' at Present in its Infancy, may by Perseverance and Management progressively arrive at such a Pitch, as to interfere essentially with the Interests of the British Manufacturers."

Second, he concluded that Edemsor's and Royle's testimony was accurate and must be brought to the immediate attention of the British government.

And in the third place, he recognized that it would be dangerous for him as consul to help Royle leave the country. The Manufacturing Society regarded all skilled workers with such "Jealousy," Royle's departure would certainly outrage them. Were they to learn the British consul had been a party to the affair, their anger might well descend upon his head. They might break into the consulate; they might vandalize; they might attack Bond, himself.

It was, of course, true that, when acknowledging Bond's commission, the Pennsylvania government granted him all the "Privileges, Pre-Eminences, and Authority which the Laws of Nations give to a Consul." Although the phrase sounded impressive, Bond knew it signified little. For every scholar who argued that international law rendered the consul's person, offices, and mails inviolate, there was another who questioned whether the law of nations even extended to consuls.[20] The only clear "rights, privileges, and immunities" a consul enjoyed were those spelled out in a particular consular convention or commercial treaty. Between Britain and America no such document existed.

Furthermore, Bond was unclear what course he should follow. Months before he had asked the foreign office for instructions about how to handle distressed nationals, but no directives had yet reached him. He must depend on his own judgment; he must decide whether Henry Royle was worth a "personal Risque."

Although a cautious man, Bond was no coward. On the 14th of November, he called Edemsor and Royle to his office and had them make a deposition, bringing in everything they knew about the "American Seduction of British Machines and Artisans." Under oath the two Englishmen repeated the story of the Phillips machines . . . described Joseph Hague's activities . . . told how Governor Randolph of Virginia tried to persuade Royle to settle in that State . . . how the Governor tried to buy carding machines and spinners from Royle . . . how the Philadelphia house of Stuart & Barr lately brought over a Scot from Glasgow who knew how to make "Jennys" . . . and how Stuart & Barr were planning to invest twelve thousand pounds to establish the cotton business in Philadelphia.[21]

After the clerk took down the sixteen-hundred word statement, Bond turned to Royle and promised to get him out of the country. From his own purse Bond lent Royle money, booked passage for him and family with Capt. W. Keith; and, on the 21st of December, saw the Royles safely on board the *Cyrus,* bound for Cork and Liverpool.[22] Bond had saved a textile worker for the mills of Britain, but at what cost?

When the Manufacturing Society learned of Royle's escape they were furious. They raged against Bond; they rebuked him; they reviled him; they insulted him. Then the merchants joined the chorus and what Bond, in his restrained manner, called "a considerable Murmur" became a clamor.

For just after the *Cyrus* sailed, Bond uncovered a mercantile fraud. Some Philadelphia traders had illicitly obtained a set of British papers for one of their vessels. It was the old double-paper trick. The ship posed as being British in English ports and American in United States waters in order to avoid paying alien-shipping duties. By an extraordinary stroke of luck Bond got hold of the British papers, confiscated them, and infuriated the ship's owners.

The merchants joined the manufacturers in denouncing the British consul; whether they would stop with verbal attacks remained a moot question. Bond was afraid they would go further and at the very least, attack his mail. The Manufacturing Society, he was convinced, would go to great lengths to keep dispatches about their activities from reaching London and, he believed, the traders would use "every Stratagem . . . to regain the Ship's Papers."[23] With his person and his letters endangered, Bond took the only sensible course; he fled.

At the end of Christmas week, he was in New York City. He personally placed his dispatches on a British merchant ship bound for London, and then waited for tempers to cool in the City of Brotherly Love.

By the end of January 1788, Philadelphians had lost interest in the British consul; their attention was fixed on whether to adopt or reject the new federal constitution. Bond was able to return to the city without encountering any unpleasantness. Back at the consulate, he too became engrossed in the great debate that was shaping up over the constitution. Much as he feared the potential economic strength of the United States, he favored political strength; for in the final analysis Bond's heart belonged to the London merchants. His chances for collecting their debts depended on a central government "whose Energy," as he put it, "may correct the present relaxed Situation of the Laws, and restore public Faith and private Credit, . . ."[24]

The possibilities of collecting the debts remained as remote as ever. In February, for instance, the mails brought a copy of Virginia's new law, repealing previous legislation that impeded the collection of debts, *providing* Great Britain delivered up the northwest posts and made compensation for Negroes carried off during the Revolution. To Bond that piece of legislation meant that Virginia planned never to pay the debts and thoroughly justified Britain's retention of the posts. "For England," wrote Bond, "at least in the present State of public Affairs here, can have no Reliance upon the Faith of Treaties, and can not, in policy, relinquish the only Security left to compel the Observance of solemn Stipulations."[25] A few weeks later, Bond heard there was a move in South Carolina to extend the installment plan for payment of debts from three to five years and to compel creditors to accept land in payment instead of sterling.

The news discouraged the consul. In an official capacity there was nothing he could do for the British merchants; at the same time, he was so conscientious by nature that he felt it improper for him to act in a private capacity for English merchant houses. Offers to accept powers of attorney came from London; Bond turned them down.[26]

Still he did what he could. He utilized the family friendship with Benjamin Franklin, and, in March, received permission to appear before the Supreme Executive Council of Pennsylvania to plead the case for the British merchants. Council gave him, Bond thought, "a very patient and attentive Hearing." He left hoping that Pennsylvania might repeal all legislation impeding the collection of debts and that "might inspire other States" to follow suit.[27]

By then Bond had been in the United States for sixteen months. He had established a consulate and had sent the foreign office over thirty dispatches. In return, there was nothing: not one letter, not one directive, not one instruction from "My Lord Carmarthen." At times deep depression seized Bond and doubts assailed him. Was he forgotten? Was his performance poor? Were his dispatches useless? Had they arrived? Why had the foreign office failed to write?

There were days during these sixteen months when Bond could hardly endure the uncertainty. Yet his self-restraint was so much a part of him, he must bear his tribulations in silence. Only once did he break down and reveal something of his innermost feelings. In a letter to William Frazer, the under-secretary of state, Bond wrote:

> . . . it would be satisfactory to me, to hear officially, that the particular Drift of my Communications were deemed useful, and approved by Government. Not being very conversant with Matters of this Sort, my Inquiries may have been ill-applied, and the Effect of them fruitless. Hitherto, they have been directed by my own Judgment merely; I may have pursued an erroneous Plan, and, unless I receive the Instructions of Government, I may persist in improper Investigations, when apt Directions might make me make such as might be important:—I shall most faithfully observe the least Hint that may be suggested; and every Exertion shall be used to improve it.[28]

It was a piteous plea and an embarrassing admission of igno-
rance about the office. Yet there was no need for Bond to be
ashamed. No one in Britain had taken the trouble to define consular duties and every consul at the beginning of his tour encountered
the same doubts and the same sense of insecurity, for Whitehall
persisted in sending out untrained men without providing written,
general instructions for their guidance.[29] The consular service—as
Bond discovered—remained in a state of suspended adolescence.

Later he reveled in the opportunities offered to help mold
and organize the service, but, until he learned from experience, he
suffered from having to work in the dark. "As my Duties were not
defined," he later told a friend, "I felt the Possibility of trespassing
upon Grounds, which it was never mean't I should explore—and I
apprehended the Danger of innovating particular Lines of Duty,
assigned to Others, & expected from Them:—Had my Line of
Duty been chalked out, I should have been more at Ease. . . ."[30]

But the worst was nearly over. At the end of April 1788,
Bond sent a short letter to Carmarthen, warning against the importation of American wheat because of the prevalence of an insect,
called the Hessian fly.[31] In August, a letter arrived from Carmarthen! It tersely stated that an order-in-council prohibited the
importation of American wheat until "His Majesty's Pleasure shall
be further signified," and instructed Bond to make a study of the
Hessian fly, "and the Damage done thereby to the Wheat."[32]

It was not the kind of letter for which Bond had been looking,
but it was better than nothing. He threw himself heart and soul into
collecting the required information. On horseback, a mode of
travel he never enjoyed, he rode through Chester, Lancaster, Berks,
and Montgomery counties observing crop conditions; he collected
studies on the Hessian fly and forwarded them to the foreign
office.[33] Ironically, for it was not a topic that interested him, he
became an authority on the subject; excerpts of his dispatches were
published in the third edition of the *Encyclopedia Britannica*.

Meanwhile, Bond kept abreast of the constitutional crisis. On
May 5th, he wrote that "Maryland has, by a very large Majority,
adopted the new Form of Government" . . . on June 28th; "New
Hampshire had adopted the Federal Constitution:—this being the

9th State . . . it is presumed immediate Measures will be taken to convene a Congress" . . . On August 3rd; "Within a few Days, the Convention of New York have ratified the Federal Constitution" . . . And on October 2nd; "It is most probable, my Lord, the new Federal Constitution will be put in Motion in the Course of the Spring."[34]

The reports on the adoption of the constitution marked the end of Bond's period of insecurity. As the federal government came into being, the British took a new look at the United States of America and at their consul in Philadelphia.

NOTES

[1]Bond to Evan Nepean, under-secretary of state, Philadelphia, November 16, 1788, *AHAAR*, 1896, I, 589. Upon learning of George Hammond's appointment as Britain's first minister to the United States, Bond wrote to Lord Grenville that "The Correspondence I have necessarily taken upon myself, in the Absence of a Minister, will soon devolve into more experienced Hands. . . ." Philadelphia, October 8, 1791, *AHAAR*, 1897, 491–492.

[2]*United States Census, 1790, Heads of Families, Pennsylvania*, p. 238.

[3]See statement of Humes & Etting, auctioneers in CAD COLL, PB, "Vouchers-Personal" Box for a fairly complete listing of Bond's personal property; also statements of the Phoenix Assurance Co., London, England in "Misc. Legal" Box. Bond carried $7900.00 worth of insurance on his household goods, which included $1500.00 on books and $800.00 on china. For the total policy he paid an annual premium of $29.62.

[4]Beef cost Bond 8*d* a pound . . . 6 tongues £1-2-6 . . . a leg of mutton £3-2½ . . . 4½ lbs. of lamb £-2-3 . . . 4 dozen bottles of Claret £9— . . . 1 pipe of London Madeira, bought from Thomas Giese in Philadelphia, £45— . . . 1 cask of Jamaica coffee and 1 cask of Jamaica sugar cost £15-3-9. See vouchers in CAD COLL, PB, "Vouchers-Personal" Box.

[5]See invoices from Charles Dilly from 1786–1793, "Vouchers-Personal" Box.

[6]William Havard to Bond, London, August 14, 1788, CAD COLL, PB, "H-L" Box.

[7]On November 3, 1788 Bond bought "a Grey Horse warranted sound" from James Starn for £12—; on November 15, 1788 he exchanged a bay pony with J. Taylor for a bay horse. "Vouchers-Personal" Box.

[8]On October 24, 1788 Ann Warder wrote in her diary: "Phineas Bond called, the latter now considered a great man here." "Extracts from the Diary of Ann Warder," Sarah Cadbury, ed. *PMHB*, XVIII, 63.

[9]See, for instance, Dr. Shippen's description of "an elegant tea party" given by his daughter, Nancy, in a letter to "Tommy," Philadelphia, June 1, 1789, Nancy Shippen, *Nancy Shippen her Journal Book, The International Romance of a Young Lady of Fashion of Colonial Philadelphia*, Esther Ames, ed. (Philadelphia, 1935), p. 249. Also see Elizabeth Drinker, *Extracts from the Journal of Elizabeth Drinker, from 1759 to 1809*, Henry D. Biddle, ed. (Philadelphia, 1889), pp. 46, 53, 79; and invitations to Bond and "The Misses Bond" from Mrs. Penn for tea and musical parties in CAD COLL, PB, "Vouchers" Box.

[10]Quoted by Robert Fynn, *British Consuls Abroad: Their Origin, Rank, Privileges, Duties, Jurisdiction, and Emoluments; Including the Laws, Orders in Council, and Instructions by Which They are Governed* (2nd ed., London, 1849), p. 41.

[11]When George Canning was secretary of state for foreign affairs, he tried in 1825 and again in 1826 to restrict British consuls from trading. The directives were comparatively effective with the exception of vice-consuls, many of whom received no salary. In 1835, consuls testifying before a parliamentary committee unanimously agreed that Canning's restrictions had been beneficial and as a result British consuls received preferential treatment at foreign courts over American consuls who were engaged in business enterprises. See in particular the testimony of James Henderson, Esq., consul general at Bogota, *British Sessional Papers, House of Commons, 1835,* Edgar L. Erickson, ed. (London, 1835), VI, 162–169.

[12]Sworn deposition of Thomas Edemsor and Henry Royle, November 14, 1787, before P. Bond, Consul, enclosure in Bond to Carmarthen, November 20, 1787, FO 4/5.

[13]One spinner was a Hallwood with 64 spindles or threads; the two others were "Jennys" with 60 and 44 spindles respectively.

[14]The most detailed account of the Manufacturing Society remains that by J. Leander Bishop, *A History of American Manufactures from 1608 to 1860* (Philadelphia, 1864), I, 404–411.

[15]Bond to Carmarthen, Philadelphia, November 20, 1787, *AHAAR,* 1896, I, 554.

[16]Bond to Carmarthen, Philadelphia, March 30, 1788, *AHAAR,* 1896, I, 564; *Pennsylvania Gazette,* March 19, 1788.

[17]Bond to Carmarthen, Philadelphia, November 20, 1787, *AHAAR,* 1896, I, 553.

[18]See in particular articles in the *Pennsylvania Gazette* for March 19, 1788, June 25, 1788, and August 6, 1788.

[19]Bond to Carmarthen, Philadelphia, November 16, 1788, *AHAAR,* 1896, I, 581.

[20]Emirich de Vattel's opinion was that "The Sovereign, by the very act of receiving him [i.e., the consul] tacitly engages to allow him all the liberty and safety necessary to the proper discharge of his functions. . . ." Wicquefort, on the other hand, questioned whether consuls enjoy the protection of the law of nations and so did Jefferson in his early years as American secretary of state. See Emirich de Vattel, *The Law of Nations, or Principles of the Law of Nature Applied to the Conduct and Affairs of Nations and Sovereigns,* Joseph Chitty, ed. (Philadelphia, 1859), pp. 147–148; Graham H. Stuart, *American Diplomatic and Consular Practice* (New York, 1936), p. 430.

[21]FO 4/5.

[22]Bond to Carmarthen, Philadelphia, December 29, 1787, *AHAAR,* 1896, I, 556–557.

[23]Bond to Carmarthen, New York, January 2, 1788, and Philadelphia, February 3, 1788, *AHAAR,* 1896, I, 557, 558.

[24]Bond to Carmarthen, Philadelphia, March 3, 1788, *AHAAR,* 1896, I, 559.

[25]Bond to Carmarthen, Philadelphia, March 3, 1788, *AHAAR,* 1896, I, 560.

[26]Havard to Bond, London, August 14, 1788, CAD COLL, PB, "H-L" Box.

[27]See Bond to Benjamin Franklin, 2nd Street, March 7, 1788, *Pennsylvania Archives,* XI, 255; Minutes of the Supreme Executive Council of Pennsylvania, March 10, 1788 and March 12, 1788, *Colonial Records,* XV, 408, 410; Bond to Carmarthen, Philadelphia, March 30, 1788, *AHAAR,* 1896, I, 561–562.

[28]Philadelphia, October 1, 1787, *AHAAR,* 1896, I, 550.

[29]See recommendations to Select Parliamentary Committee on Consular Establishment, July 16, 1835, *British Sessional Papers,* VI, 169–170.

[30]Bond to James Bland Burges, Esq., Philadelphia, April 12, 1791, The Burges Papers, Bodleian Library, Oxford University, Oxford, England, by courtesy of Mrs. F. Morris-Davies, 6 Hayward Road, Oxford, England.

[31]Bond to Carmarthen, Philadelphia, April 22, 1788, *AHAAR,* 1896, I, 565–566.

[32]Carmarthen to Bond, Whitehall, June 26, 1788, PRO, FO 4/6.

[33]Bond to Carmarthen, Philadelphia, October 1, 1788, *AHAAR,* 1896, I, 572–577 and enclosures, FO 4/6; enclosures in Bond to Carmarthen, Philadelphia, October 1, 1788 and October 2, 1788, FO 4/6; Bond to Carmarthen, Philadelphia, November 3, 1788, *AHAAR,* 1896, I, 579–581.

[34]*AHAAR,* 1896, I, 566, 567, 569, 578.

CHAPTER SEVEN

*Working for the
Committee of Trade*

In London, at the beginning of 1789, it seemed that the constitutional crisis in America was coming to an end without the
country breaking into several distinct parts. By then Whitehall had
received a report from Bond that two-thirds of the states had ratified the new constitution and that it would most probably "be put
into Motion in the Course of the Spring."[1] The foreign department
had studied the document—a copy of which Bond had sent the
moment the convention rose.[2] It was clear the new federal government would be far stronger than its predecessor. Instead of the
states, the central authority would henceforth regulate commerce.
Moreover, the provision for federal courts and the declaration that
treaties were to be recognized as "the supreme law of the land"
promised to expedite collection of the debts . . . perhaps even to
resolve the problem.

Propitious as the situation appeared, Carmarthen was content
to continue the policy of wait-and-see and in the meantime to play
with old lines. Projects which had failed with the first government
of the Free United States might succeed with the second. His
thoughts turned again to his favorite solution for the impasse over
diplomatic representation: British commissaries for commercial
affairs.

On February 4, 1789, the secretary of state broke his long
silence and wrote a personal letter to Phineas Bond. The first paragraph read in part as follows:

Whitehall, February 4, 1789

Sir:
    Your Letters dated the 4th of last month arrived this Morn-
ing, and I would not defer acknowledging the Receipt of them by

the Mail of today as the very clear and able Manner in which you have expressed Yourself . . . appears to be very deserving of my entire Approbation. If however the New Constitution should finally be adopted, it appears to me to be very proper that you should present your Commission as His Majesty's Commissary for all Commercial Affairs for Approbation and I am persuaded you will not omit anything which will be in your Power to promote the Interests of those Persons who have just Claims on the Subjects of the United States.[3]

A month later Carmarthen wrote again instructing Bond to resubmit his commission. Although it was customary to send duplicate instructions, the second letter contained a note of urgency that had been absent in the first. "You will not," Carmarthen directed Bond, "lose any Time in using your utmost Endeavours to obtain your Recognition in that Character [i.e., commissary for commercial affairs]."[4]

The letters reached Philadelphia during March and April, and quite contrary to his habits Bond let three months pass before acknowledging their receipt. Although they contained that once longed-for phrase, "my entire Approbation," the directives failed to restore the eroded edge of the consul's enthusiasm. It was obvious Carmarthen still thought of him as commissary rather than as consul. Unlike the Secretary of State, Bond seriously doubted that the new American government would assume any different attitude toward British commissaries than had the Continental Congress.

By the time the second instruction arrived, the federal government had, indeed, formed in New York City: George Washington was president; John Adams, vice-president; behind closed doors the new senate was engaged in acrimonious debate over executive titles; the new house of representatives in public session was threatening to erect an American navigation system operative against Great Britain; but in spite of all the innovations, John Jay remained foreign secretary. He had rejected the commissary commission once; Bond was certain he would reject it again. Only if Washington were to appoint a new secretary could Bond see any chance of raising the office, like Lazarus, from the dead. And so he deliberately ignored the letter of his instructions. He put Carmarthen off with the statement that while the public departments were "in a Train of being arranged," he thought "it adviseable to postpone my Application for some little Time."[5]

Bond had changed. Two and a half years on the job had toughened him. Two and a half years of Carmarthen's neglect had lowered the Secretary of State in his estimation. Literary praise from the Marquis was no longer enough; now Bond wanted financial reward.

Five times he had written Carmarthen requesting an expense account.[6] He even had two London merchant friends, Martin Petrie and Robert Barclay, lobby on his behalf. Although they were partially successful in that Carmarthen did submit to the treasury lords a request for "contingent Expenses" for Mr. Bond, the Lords turned it down. Such expenditures, they claimed, must come from the privy purse. "I fear," Petrie wrote Bond, "we must now apply to mr. pitt [sic]—assure yourself what can, shall be done."[7] But these words made for cold comfort; like everyone else connected with government Bond knew how careful Pitt was about dipping into the privy purse.

Then again Bond had written three times for the right to charge consulage.[8] These were fees consuls collected for routine services such as administering oaths, opening wills, and registering and certifying documents. British consuls to the Barbaries continually collected consulage, but Whitehall had never indicated whether those serving in America might do so. In the absence of specific instructions Miller, the consul at Charleston, South Carolina, and Temple as well as Bond passed by the customary emoluments of the office.

Yet Bond was reaching the point where he could no longer continue to live like a minister on a consul's salary. He must have additional money from some source. In August he would be forty —a dangerous age to face retrenchment and the surrender of comforts. Bond recalled how he had skimped during the years of exile, and he felt now too old to become again pennywise. He was in this frame of mind when the worst blow of all fell.

In May 1789, Bond received a letter from his agent in London, Mr. J. Sneyd, who wrote that the treasury lords, considering Bond's appointment under the Crown sufficient compensation, had ruled against his claim for losses as an "American Sufferer."[9] That was the final straw. It broke the back of Bond's high resolves.

For thirty months he had refused all offers to act as attorney. The consular post, he thought, deserved his full attention. Furthermore, he believed it was fundamentally immoral for public servants to engage on the side in private businesses. Still he must have money, and every proper channel for procuring it had failed. After Sneyd's letter came, Bond succumbed.

At the end of May he was in Richmond interviewing David Ross and Thomas Pleasants, Jr., tobacco dealers who owned large sums to Bond's merchant friends. With the Virginians Bond entered into what he described as "a very full Investigation of the Subject" of the debts. "But," he wrote to William Havard, the London merchant, "as I had no special Authority from the Brit: Creds. to come to any Conclusion . . . I could only enter as it were into some sort of Preliminary Treaty."[10] In other words, he invited an active agency. That was precisely what Havard had been waiting for.

Bond later learned that the moment his letter arrived, Havard called a meeting at the George and Vulture Tavern in Cornhill of the sixty-one creditors of Ross, Pleasants and Hay Co. They agreed to work as a whole and unanimously voted to have Phineas Bond, Esq. act as their collective agent with full powers of attorney.[11] News that His Majesty's consul in Philadelphia would now accept active agencies spread through London's mercantile circles. Other cases followed. By the end of the year Bond's financial crisis was over.

By then he had also mapped out in his mind the course of action he would follow in collecting the debts. It became for him a classic pattern. Before accepting a case Bond insisted the creditors agree to act as a unit. Next, he tried always to settle out of court. Aware of what he described as the "monstrous Delays" in the courts of "this wretched Country," handling the cases without resorting to litigation seemed "the most speedy, the most effectual & least expensive mode of satisfying the demands of the Brit. Creds." Instead of suing, he tried to work out with the debtors a feasible plan for payment. In the Ross, Pleasants & Hay case, for instance, Bond drew up an indenture between himself and Ross and Pleasants which provided for the payment of their total debt of £36,951-9- sterling in six annual installments. The first was due on May 12, 1791. In case of default Ross and Pleasants agreed to pay two installments after eight months passed, one on which the default was made and the next in order of succession.[12]

If the worst came to the worst and the debtors continually defaulted, then Bond attempted to get hold of their land. That proved an effective but slow means of realizing the debts. As Bond discovered, it took time to sell tracts of land which often were located in the wilderness. In the Ross case, for example, continual defaults drove Bond to take David Ross's immense landholdings in Kentucky, Tennessee, and Ohio. The selling of the tracts was still going on when Bond died. But it always remained his conviction that land was the answer to the problem of the debts. As a result the Harrison decision jolted Bond.

Thomas Harrison, who was a citizen of Baltimore, died in 1782. In his will he left his estate to a brother, John, a member of parliament in England, and to a sister and her children in Ireland. When finally settled, the estate came to some £36,000, most of it derived from the sale of lands. The question was whether under those circumstances Harrison's relatives might inherit. In the late spring of 1789 the chancery court in Maryland handed down an adverse decision. Harrison's relatives, the court ruled, were aliens and as such were unable to inherit the money since most of it had been realized from land and since aliens might not hold real property in Maryland.[13]

At once Bond informed Carmarthen, now the fifth duke of Leeds. When Harrison died, Bond pointed out, American independence was not yet recognized and legally "the Inhabitants of both Countries were the Subjects of England." He also argued that the ruling contravened the provision for "mutual Enjoyment of Rights" in the peace treaty. But there was even more to the Harrison decision, and Bond spotted the deeper ramifications. In his own words:

> I am well aware, my Lord, that if both my Commissions were recognized in their fullest Scope by the United States, my Author-

ity would not be deemed competent to represent a Matter of this Nature, and enable me to apply for some legislative Interposition to correct this monstrous Inconvenience, being perfectly foreign to any Thing of a commercial Kind.[14]

In short, Bond was reaching the conclusion that neither consuls nor commissaries could adequately represent Great Britain in the United States. It was becoming his conviction that His Majesty must send a minister to America. A few months later his position on this point became more firmly fixed.

In August, no longer able to ignore Carmarthen's instructions, Bond went to New York. He waited upon Jay. Again Bond pressed for recognition as commissary for commercial affairs; as he had foreseen, again Jay turned him down.[15]

Nonetheless, since he was in New York, Bond made the most of his visit. He saw old friends, among them George Clymer who was now a member of the house of representatives. Bond spent some time with Clymer and other congressmen. They tried to impress upon the British consul that the United States had a "regularized Government" which would honor "compacts with foreign Powers" and so the time had arrived for the conclusion of an Anglo-American commercial treaty. They made it equally clear that what they wanted from a treaty was the opening of the British West Indies to American shipping.

Bond remained unconvinced about the Indies. Mercantilist that he was, he believed as an island kingdom Great Britain's very existence depended upon retaining a monopoly of the world's carrying trade. In the United States, Bond saw a potential rival. He explained the situation in the following manner:

—the People of New England are an enterprizing People . . . They navigate their Vessels frugally and their Outfits are infinitely less expensive than the Outfits of British Vessels. When once admitted to trade with the West India Islands, Shipbuilding, which has lain dormant almost, and which was formerly a Source of great Profit to this Country, would instantly be revived—Americans would soon monopolize the Advantages of Carrying; . . . the Numbers of her Vessels would be increased, and by increasing the Numbers would supply the Means of conveying all the Products of America, which are consumed in our Islands, and that too at a much cheaper Rate than any other Nation could afford. But the enterprizing Spirit of the People of New England would, as soon as they found the Channels of Profit open, be exerted to the Raising a maritime Force, which, in a case of a future War, might operate very detrimentally to the Interests of England. The Trade to our Islands would afford America a productive Nursery for Seamen, and at least diminish, if not eventually annihilate that *Nursery,* which the present Commerce of Great Britain with the United States, afford in no slight degree.[16]

Provided the Indies remained shut to the Americans, Bond agreed with the congressmen about a commercial treaty. He was, in his own words, for promoting "any Plan that might be conducive to the facilitating Remittances and Diminishing that Load of Debt, which the People of these States owe to the Brit. Merchants." Were a treaty to be negotiated, then a minister must be sent to the United States. Bond laid these thoughts before the British secretary of state.[17]

Months before his dispatch reached London, the Duke of Leeds had arrived at similar conclusions. On May 24, 1789, he had received a letter from Philadelphia that summarized the debate in the house of representatives over customs duties. Enclosed were Madison's speeches in which he urged congress to place discriminatory duties on goods and tonnage from countries who had no commercial treaties with the United States—in other words, from Great Britain.[18] As Leeds saw it, the passing of such a measure would inevitably lead to an Anglo-American commercial war. Clearly, the time had come to reevaluate British policy toward the United States.

At once Leeds raised the question with the Committee of Trade. As far as America was concerned, the foreign department never altered policy without first gaining the assent of the powerful Lords of Trade. Leeds presented the committee with a copy of Bond's dispatch. Almost immediately that body agreed to study all facets of the American economy.

On the 9th of June, the lords "ordered that a Letter be written to His Majesty's Consuls & to any other persons His Grace may think proper residing in the . . . United States of America, directing them after having made the fullest Enquiry to report in as accurate a manner as possible" on eleven, specific points.[19]

On the 30th of June, Leeds completed and sent to Miller, Temple, and Bond a lengthy instruction. It included all of the committee's questions and commanded the consuls to make "the fullest Enquiries" and report "as accurately as possible" on the following matters "for the Information of the . . . Privy Council for Trade."

The first three questions reflected the concern over possible discrimination against British goods and vessels requesting, as they did, exact figures on American customs duties and stressing the importance of reporting any differences that might exist. The committee wanted to know whether British vessels coming to the United States paid the same port duties as other foreign vessels; whether there were any differences in the taxes imposed on the goods and commodities from Great Britain and those from other European countries; whether there was any discrimination against cargoes coming from British colonies and from the colonies of other countries; and whether the United States made any distinctions between goods brought in ships belonging to American citizens, British citizens, and the citizens of other foreign nations.

The seventh and eighth questions pointed up the uneasiness over the carrying trade and the fear of American competition. The directive requested figures on the number of vessels under construction in each state and on the number of vessels with their tonnage "now belonging to the Subjects of each State respectively." Had the shipping in each state, asked the instruction, been increasing or decreasing and by how much? The consuls must also provide statistics on the amount of tonnage "belonging to the different Nations of Europe, or their respective Colonies" that had annually entered the ports of the United States "since the Year 1783."

Interested in the possibility of creating an Indian barrier state in the back country, the committee requested precise information on American emigration "to the Banks of the Great Lakes, the Ohio, the Missouri and Mississippi" together with descriptions of the kinds of government that were being formed in the wilderness and the kinds of subsistence and commerce that were being pursued there.

The remaining questions dealt with the debts owed the British merchants and the current condition of American agriculture, industry, and population. The letter ended with the desire "that You will report to me any . . . Information on these Subjects which You may already have transmitted in order to bring the whole into one View."

As might be expected, the first answers came from Bond. They arrived at Whitehall at the beginning of November.[21] On Monday, the ninth, Under-Secretary of State Burges sent a transcription of Bond's report to the Committee for Trade. By Wednesday the clerks had finished copying twelve of Bond's earlier letters and these were also sent to the committee.[22] On Thursday, Leeds formalized the whole project by asking the Lords of Trade "what proposals of a commercial nature should be proper to make to the United States."[23]

For the next seventeen months the committee interviewed London and Glasgow merchants, and customs officials, and studied reports from special agents who were in America, and from the three British consuls there. Their chief source of information proved to be the reports from Bond. His were the most thorough and comprehensive. One alone, for example, amounted to thirty printed pages and contained fifty-two enclosures![24]

Although Bond covered all the questions, it was obvious from his letters that the indentured traffic in particular attracted his attention. Bond sent lists of the number of passengers arriving annually since 1783 at Philadelphia, Wilmington, Baltimore, and Charleston. The schedules gave the ships' names, their masters, tonnage, ports of departure and arrival. According to his figures 5,213 Irish, mostly indentured servants and redemptioners, came in the single year of 1789. He argued that the traffic ought to be controlled. He played upon the humanitarian feelings of the Committee for Trade, describing the "small Vessels, destitute of proper Room and Accommodation, and abridged of the Necessary Allowance of proper Food." The ship *Nancy,* for instance, displacing only one hundred and thirty-one tons, carried from Londonderry to Philadelphia three hundred passengers on a single trip. Also Bond pointed out how the traffic increased the population of

America at the expense of the British Isles; and finally that it formed the chief means by which models of English machines and skilled British artisans were "seduced" into the United States. Bond suggested imposing regulations on passenger vessels, like those on the slave traders, which would be sufficiently stiff as to make the indentured traffic unprofitable.[25]

At the moment, the committee was more interested in the sample of maple sugar Bond sent them; for, if that manufactury developed, the United States would be less dependent upon the British West Indies.[26] Even more significant were the schedules Bond sent on American ship building, imports, and customs duties. He sent long lists on the quantities imported and duties paid on different kinds of wines, ale, porter, beer, malt, brown sugar, loaf sugar, coffee, cocoa, tallow, cheese, cordage, unwrought steel, nails and spikes, salt, snuff, indigo, coal, pickled fish and dried fish, Bohea tea, black tea, Huston tea, and other green teas. Bond also sent figures on the quantities of wheat and flour exported from Philadelphia together with the disturbing news that the revolutionary government of France had agents at all the "out Ports" to purchase flour regardless of price. "The Cargoes thus purchased," read Bond's report, "are sent to France and there disposed of at low Rates by order of Government to keep the People in Humor."[27] He suggested to the committee that they foil the French by buying up American wheat. But the Lords brushed that suggestion aside and concluded that, although "when the crops fail in Europe the United States may export great quantities . . . no trade is so precarious as that of corn, and no system of commerce permanently profitable can be founded on it."[28]

At the end of January 1791, the committee finished its study. They had a few copies printed which they regarded as highly confidential. They never troubled to send one to the consul at Philadelphia, although in the report the Lords graciously acknowledged their indebtedness to Bond and accredited him for many of the figures and statistics upon which the conclusions were drawn and which were included in the appendix.[29]

The report made it clear the Lords of Trade were well satisfied with the commercial situation. The policy of keeping American shipping out of the British West Indies had proved a success. Since the war, British imports to the islands and the Maritime Provinces had increased on an average of £166,085 per annum and "It is worthy of notice," pointed out the Lords, "that the increase has been almost wholly in British manufactures." The number of vessels engaged in the trade had also increased: to the Maritimes by "about one-half," to the West Indies by "about 1-7th." The paper went out of its way to emphasize that those ships were "built and manned in Great Britain and consequently contribute in a greater degree than the ships they have replaced to increase the efficient strength of Great Britain as a Naval power." Before the war many of the vessels in the trade "belonged to the inhabitants of the now United States; at present they can only belong to British subjects resident in the British dominions."[30] The nursery of seamen was growing.

While Anglo-American trade in general had declined, which the Lords regretted, they were at the same time pleased to find that "the value of exports to the now United States has exceeded the value of imports from thence . . . in a much greater proportion than before the war." The balance of trade between the two countries was more in favor of Great Britain than it had been. Also they were pleased to announce that British vessels in American ports outnumbered European ships four to one.[31] On the other hand, it was happily noted, American shipping had declined. Facts and figures were vindicating the committee's president, Lord Hawkesbury. Six years before in Commons, as plain Charles Jenkinson, he had prophesied that ". . . if proper means could be devised to secure the navigation trade to Great Britain, though we had lost a dominion, we might almost be said to have gained an empire."[32]

Fears previously entertained by Hawkesbury and other members had dissipated. There was no discrimination in American duties against British imports nor were any distinctions made between goods coming from the colonies and from the mother country. American duties were actually less than those imposed by "most European countries," leading the Lords to the magnanimous conclusion that "the United States being now an independent nation, Great Britain upon the whole has no right to complain. . . ."

Still, American port duties presented a problem. All foreign vessels coming into the United States paid two shillings per ton more than native vessels, but American ships in British ports paid no alien duties. Although the Lords admitted Americans must pay various landing tolls and lighthouse and pilot fees that almost counterbalanced the distinctions, they favored negotiation to eliminate the inequalities.[33]

It was now the conviction of the Lords that there was nothing to fear with respect to manufacturing. On the contrary, for years to come the United States and the back country would present a market for British products. They reported no industry south of Pennsylvania and the goods being produced in the middle and northern states were, in their own words, "inferior in quality and dearer than those" made in England. Again they assumed a generous attitude. "The inhabitants of all temperate climates," they pointed out, "will occassionally employ themselves in manufactures for domestic use. But these domestic occupations seldom give rise of manufactures of any great extent." Furthermore, "it is astonishing how much they [i.e., Americans] prefer agriculture to manufacturing."[34]

The debts were no longer a bitter issue. While calling the state laws that had impeded their recovery "unfriendly," the committee now confessed that "the late Congress used such means as were in their power to correct and prevent" them. It was almost as if His Britannic Majesty's ministers had about-faced. The whole report breathed a spirit of amiability. After all, read one sentence, "Some allowance was to be made for the resentment natural after a war of seven years. . . ." As long as the Americans were excluded from trading with British possessions in the New World, nothing could be lost by extending a welcoming hand to the United States. The Lords of Trade could see no reason now why "the people of the two countries, though no longer fellow subjects," should not be "friends, at least, as before the war."[35]

Therefore, the committee recommended opening negotiations with America for a commercial treaty in which the United States would pledge itself not to raise duties on British goods higher than those from any other foreign country, and in which the British West Indies should remain shut to American shipping.[36]

The way was clear for Whitehall to consider negotiations for a treaty and to send a British minister to the United States. But before Leeds—who never moved very quickly—got around to appointing a minister, he became entangled in a dispute with Pitt over the Russian question. In April 1791 he resigned. William Wyndham, Lord Grenville, a kinsman of the Prime Minister, became secretary of state for the foreign department.

In September, Grenville appointed his friend and protégé, George Hammond, minister plenipotentiary to the United States. The new Secretary of State also wrote to the consul at Philadelphia—now the temporary capital—informing him of Hammond's appointment and instructing him to afford the minister the fullest assistance and to pay "the strictest Attention to all such Matters as he shall, from Time to Time, communicate to You."[37]

The directive ended the first phase of Bond's consular career. The duties and correspondence, as he put it, that "I have necessarily taken upon myself in the Absence of a Minister will soon devolve into more experienced Hands"[38]—a state of affairs Bond had himself helped to bring about.

NOTES

[1]Bond to Carmarthen, Philadelphia, October 2, 1788, *AHAAR*, 1896, I, 578.

[2]Bond sent Carmarthen a copy of the constitution on September 20, 1787; it reached Whitehall on November 3, 1787, see *AHAAR*, 1896, I, 546.

[3]British Foreign Correspondence: America, Henry Adams Transcripts, Hammond, 1789–1792, Library of Congress, Washington, D.C.

[4]Carmarthen to Bond, Whitehall, March 4, 1789, FO 4/7.

[5]Bond to the Duke of Leeds, Philadelphia, June 3, 1789, *AHAAR*, 1896, I, 599.

[6]Bond wrote for additional expense money on May 15, 1787, May 30, 1787, October 1, 1787, November 4, 1787, and November 20, 1787.

[7]Martin Petrie to Bond, London, September 1, 1789, CAD COLL, Thomas Cadwalader Section, "Legal-Bond" Box.

[8]Bond wrote about consulage on October 1, 1787, November 4, 1787, and August 3, 1788.

[9]Quoted in Bond to Leeds, Philadelphia, June 2, 1789, *AHAAR*, 1896, I, 596–598.

[10]Bond to Havard, Richmond, May 8, 1789, CAD COLL, PB, "Ross" Box.

[11]Minutes of the creditors' meeting, July 7, 1789; Havard to Bond, London, October 6, 1789, CAD COLL, PB, "Ross" Box.

[12]Bond to Havard, Richmond, May 8, 1789; Indenture between Ross, Pleasants and Bond, May 12, 1790, CAD COLL, PB, "Ross" Box.

[13]A lengthy description of the case is enclosed in Bond to Leeds, Philadelphia, July 12, 1789, FO 4/7.

[14]Bond to Leeds, Philadelphia, July 12, 1789, AHAAR, 1896, I, 601.

[15]John Jay to Bond, Office for Foreign Affairs, August 24, 1789 in Bond to Leeds, Philadelphia, September 17, 1789, FO 4/7.

[16]Bond to Leeds, Philadelphia, September 12, 1789, FO 4/7.

[17]Bond to Leeds, Philadelphia, September 17, 1789, AHAAR, 1896, I, 615–616.

[18]Bond to Leeds, Philadelphia, April 29, 1789, AHAAR, 1896, I, 595–596.

[19]Minutes of the Committee for Trade, June 9, 1789, Council Chambers, Whitehall, PRO, Board of Trade 5/5.

[20]FO 4/7.

[21]Bond sent these reports on the 21st and 22nd of September 1789.

[22]BT 6/22.

[23]As quoted by Anna Lingelbach, "The Inception of the Board of Trade," AHR (July 1925), p. 719.

[24]See Bond to Leeds, Philadelphia, November 10, 1789, AHAAR, 1896, I, 621–650.

[25]See in particular Bond to Leeds, Philadelphia, November 16, 1788 and November 10, 1789, FO 4/6, 4/7.

[26]Bond to Leeds, Philadelphia, July 10, 1790, FO 4/8; Report of a Committee of the Lords of the Privy Council on the Trade of Great Britain with the United States, January 1791, Worthington C. Ford, ed. (Washington, D.C., 1888), p. 30.

[27]Bond to Leeds, March 1, 1790, AHAAR, 1897, 459–460.

[28]See Committee of Trade Report, p. 46.

[29]Committee of Trade Report, p. 22.

[30]Committee of Trade Report, p. 19.

[31]Committee of Trade Report, pp. 13, 25.

[32]The Parliamentary History of England from the Earliest Period to the Year 1808, William Cobbett, ed. (London, 1814), XXV, 1373.

[33]Committee of Trade Report, pp. 37–38.

[34]Committee of Trade Report, pp. 30–31.

[35]Committee of Trade Report, p. 44.

[36]See in particular Committee of Trade Report, pp. 13 and 42.

[37]Grenville to Bond, Whitehall, September 1791, FO 4/11.

[38]Bond to Grenville, Philadelphia, October 8, 1791, AHAAR, 1897, 491–492.

CHAPTER EIGHT

Working with the
British Minister

During the first six months of 1791, Bond was happier than he had been for some time. Problems seemed to unravel themselves; responsibilities lightened; and, what was most gratifying, friends proved true.

Robert Barclay had promised he would get Bond an expense account even if it meant applying to Pitt himself; and he did. Barclay badgered the foreign office until they awarded Bond an additional £200 sterling a year for "contingent Charges," which raised his salary to £900 per annum. At the same time, Martin Petrie, although he had given up trade for a post in the customs office, continued recommending Bond to London merchants. Through Petrie, Bond received several new briefs. Nash & Martin Co., for example, for whom Lord John Russell was collecting debts in the United States, were so impressed by Petrie's praises of the Philadelphia consul that they changed agents. Even kinsman Erskine sent Bond business. After a three-year silence, the "great man" wrote a newsy letter, boasting that he was now head of the King's Bench, earned £8,000 a year, and had four sons and four daughters. Enclosed was a case that turned out to be both complicated and lucrative.[1]

As a result of the increases in salary and legal fees, Bond no longer worried about money. He was now "well satisfied," as he put it, with his financial situation. Then too he had become a matchmaker.

For the past eighteen years—since the death of his father—Bond had been head of the family. Except for the brief period when Williamina was married to General John Cadwalader, there was no one with whom he could share the responsibility. His sisters, although handsome, were slow to find husbands. In 1791, Frances, the youngest, was already twenty-three; neither she, nor Elizabeth, nor Rebecca had married. Williamina, the eldest, was thirty-eight, and like her mother appeared perfectly contented to remain a widow. Bond did all he could for the ladies. He escorted them to teas and dances; he introduced them to every eligible Englishman who came to town. He was, in fact, an ideal brother, and perhaps too much so; for the preoccupation with the family largely explained why Bond was himself still single.

At last one of his sisters fell in love. It was Elizabeth. Through Phineas, she met John Travis, a wealthy merchant who had recently arrived from England with plans to settle in Philadelphia. Travis was likeable. He was gregarious. He proposed. On March 27, 1791, at Christ's Church, Bond had the pleasure of giving Elizabeth away in holy matrimony to John Travis. His family responsibilities were reduced by one.[2]

Two weeks later, his consular responsibilities eased. Early in April, Colonel John Hamilton, a former American Loyalist, waited upon Bond—as once Bond had waited upon Sir John Temple—to submit his credentials as George III's consul for Virginia together with James Patton's commission as vice-consul for the "Potowmack." This time the interview was pleasant from beginning to end. The importance of Norfolk as a port had been brought home to Bond when he was collecting data for the Lords of Trade. He then learned that British bottoms accounted for seven-eighths of the shipping there. He also found out how difficult it was, in the absence of British consuls, to get accurate figures and statistics from Virginia. Obliged to rely on private citizens, on factors, and on merchants, he rapidly reached the conclusion that "in no one State," as he wrote to Leeds, "is the Superintendence of a Person of judgement, activity, ability, and address deemed more requisite."[3] That the foreign office had filled the vacancies flattered Bond. He was equally pleased to learn that simultaneous with Hamilton's appointment Whitehall had commissioned Thomas McDonogh as consul for Massachusetts. With Miller at Charleston, Hamilton at Norfolk, Patton at Alexandria, Bond at Philadelphia, Temple at New York, and Mc-Donogh at Boston the British consular service was firmly established in the United States. Bond had been the second consul; now there were six.

At the same time, the problem of the debts appeared to be untangling. The federal courts were finally functioning; and in state after state they were overruling, in favor of the British creditors, decisions of the lower courts. It looked to Bond as though his work was nearly done.

Although he must have known it was Whitehall's custom to leave consuls at their original place, often in the same rank, until removed by death, he always regarded his own appointment as temporary. Never for a moment did he consider remaining consul at Philadelphia for the rest of his life. On the contrary, Bond looked upon the consulship as a prelude to a diplomatic career. Surmising—quite correctly—that changes were imminent in Anglo-American relations, he felt the stir of ambition; he began to dream. Ignorant of Hammond's appointment, Bond saw himself as His Britannic Majesty's first minister to the United States! Timidly, he made a bid for the post.

On the 12th of April, he sent a confidential, carefully worded letter to Under-Secretary of State James Bland Burges. They had never met, but they had a mutual friend in Robert Barclay. Bond's excuse for writing was to thank Burges "for the very liberal Assurances you have given my kind Friend Mr. Barclay, and for the frequent Extention of good Offices, he has experienced from you, in my Behalf." The letter then reviewed the reasons for Bond's appointment, the difficulties he had encountered working for so long without guidance and without being recognized as commissary for commercial affairs, and concluded with the following paragraph:

Feeling, as I do, that my Exertions in Behalf of Individuals are gradually declining, & knowing how circumscribed my official duty is, I find I shall soon have very little Employment; which to me would be a most irksome Situation: It is my Wish to move in a more active Sphere: And while I repeat my Gratitude for your generous Assurances of Attention and Support, I beg Leave to declare You can not serve me more essentially, than by recommending Me to some efficient Pursuit, in which I can acquit myself satisfactorily.[4]

Unaware of the events transpiring at Whitehall, Bond dreamed on. High seas and gale force winds even permitted him an additional two months' grace. Normally, the April mail would have reached Philadelphia by the end of May. But the packet *Dashwood* encountered such a rough crossing, Bond only learned about Leed's resignation at the end of July.[5] Then his hopes plummeted. His patron was gone. Now there was no one at Whitehall who knew Phineas Bond personally. Under-Secretary Frazer had retired in 1789. The present under-secretaries, Burges and Aust, had never laid eyes on the Philadelphia consul.[6] To Lord Grenville he would mean no more than a signature at the end of a dispatch. Then too, the new Secretary of State would have his own friends and protégés for whom he must find places.

But Bond had tasted disappointment before and this time, because of that fortuitous letter he had written Burges, it was short-lived. In August, the Under-Secretary wrote assuring Bond he had nothing to fear from Grenville. His Lordship was fair-minded and had already formed a high opinion of Bond's work. Having served on the Committee for Trade, Grenville was well acquainted with Bond's reports and considered they had proved "of material advantage to this country." Indeed, the new Secretary of State evaluated Bond to be precisely what he was: a first-rate consul. "I have reason to believe," read Burges' letter, "that his Lordship thinks as favorably of you as you can wish."[7]

In the same letter Burges confidentially informed Bond of George Hammond's appointment as minister plenipotentiary to the United States. Since Philadelphia was the temporary capital, Hammond would reside there. After five years as an independent agent, Bond must adjust to being under immediate supervision and control. Nothing he could find out about the new minister reassured him. Hammond was only twenty-eight years old. He was one of Grenville's favorite protégés and was described as being "tall, plump, rosey-faced," but "cold and condescending in his manner;" a stiff-backed Englishman from "a very good family."[8] That description coupled with the usual ministerial attitude toward consuls augured ill for the future relationship.

Administratively, there was no separation between the diplomatic and consular services. The officers in each sent their reports directly to the secretary of state and received their instructions from him. But, technically, the services were distinct. Socially, they were poles apart. While diplomats almost inevitably came from the upper classes, consuls, for the most part, had been "in trade." Because of the gap in station, one British minister, for instance, refused to sleep under the same roof with his consul. Another had the consul assaulted in order "to put a public disgrace upon him."[9] Admittedly, these were exceptional cases. Nonetheless, as Bond well knew, ministers tended to look down upon consuls.

Still, Bond possessed certain advantages. As a barrister he stood a rung higher on the social ladder than the average consul. In Philadelphia, his family were "society." He was in the enviable position of being able to introduce Hammond to the right people and to see he received invitations from the first houses. But by nature he was too wary to rely entirely upon his assets. Long before the minister arrived, Bond had planned his strategy.

There was first the matter of a residence. Burges asked Bond to rent a furnished house for Hammond until he could look around and provide for himself. It was a routine assignment and, on the surface, appeared simple enough. Actually, it was almost impossible to fulfill. Since the previous year, when the federal workers poured into Philadelphia, houses had disappeared from the market; rents had doubled; even half-way decent lodgings were as hard to come by as the proverbial hen's teeth. Had the situation been different, Bond would not have been in the city. The problem of working with Hammond would have belonged to Temple, for as consul general he should reside at the capital. But after a six-months' unsuccessful search for a house, Temple had elected to stay in New York.[10]

Under these circumstances and anxious to avoid unpleasantnesses, Bond moved to his mother's on Union Street so that Hammond might have No. 164 Second Street. The former consulate was entirely suitable. It had been functioning, to all intents and purposes, as an embassy; and unless Hammond were a very mean man, indeed, he must appreciate the generosity of the gesture. The move might, in fact, place the minister under an obligation to the consul.

Next, Bond resolved not to force himself upon Hammond, but instead, as soon as the minister arrived, to put in for a leave of absence.[11] He wanted, in any event, to go to London. He needed to visit an optometrist, for his eyes were feeling the strain of forty-two years; some of his clients were anxious to confer with him; and for a promotion he ought to press his case in person at the foreign office. If the furlough were granted, Bond would leave in the spring—only seasoned sailors and fools dared to cross the Atlantic during the winter—and that would mean about six months of work with Hammond. For such a short period the minister and the consul should be able to get along.

Hammond arrived in the city on the 20th of October 1791, accompanied by Edward Thornton, the legation's secretary, and by a *valet de chambre* and a groom. Bond met the party and escorted them to the house on Second Street, which evidently satisfied Hammond; for there he remained, using it as both home and office, during his tour. What had been the first British consulate in Philadelphia became the first British embassy in the United States of America.

On the following day, the 21st, Bond called on Thomas Jefferson, who had succeeded Jay as American secretary of state, and explained that the minister from his country had arrived but would produce his credentials only when the United States named or invested "some Person" as minister to Great Britain.[12] Jefferson expressed his pleasure at "this favorable omen" on the part of the court of London "to cultivate harmony and good will between the two nations." He anticipated no difficulty nor delay about American reciprocation, "except if a Gentleman should be thought of who lived in a distant part of the Continent."[13]

And so, for the next three weeks, until Thomas Pinckney was named minister to the Court of St. James, Hammond posed as an ordinary visitor. Bond took full advantage of the interval. He showed Hammond around the city and the neighboring countryside, where the fall colors struck the minister "as the most magnificent" he had ever seen. He introduced Hammond to his family and friends. Their wealth, their refinement, and their intimate knowledge of England surprised Hammond and led him to suspect that most of the leading families were "Tories at heart."[14] But, in spite of this happy discovery, the minister remained uncomfortable in democratic America; cool and aloof, at times, even priggish.

Although Hammond was young and prejudiced, and ever conscious of his place and class, he could hardly have been more considerate of Mr. Bond. The minister went out of his way to be helpful and kind. Early in December, for instance, he spent an evening with George Beckwith, Grenville's unofficial agent in America. Beckwith, who was preparing to leave for England, let it slip that he expected to be back soon . . . as consul general! Hammond was shocked. It seemed to him that no one but Bond ought to succeed Sir John "both on the fair ground of regular succession and as the well deserved Reward of great and acknowledged Services." He immediately alerted Under-Secretary Burges, who, by the following packet, wrote that he could not guess upon what "that Gentleman," Beckwith, founded his expectations, but now he had "the Hint," he would "not neglect to support" Bond "in opposition to any Attempt which may be made to supplant" him.[15]

Instead of strained relations, the minister and the consul worked hand-in-glove. Hammond supported Bond's thesis about the dangers inherent in the "British Rage for Migration" and three times wrote Grenville urging the adoption of Bond's plan for a passenger act to curtail the traffic in indentured servants and redemptioners.[16] Bond, on the other hand, gave Hammond unstinted use of his knowledge and experience.

In the middle of December, Hammond received a short memorial from Jefferson, presenting the American position with respect to British contravention of the peace treaty, and asking Hammond to specify "the particular acts" which His Britannic Majesty considered as "non-compliance on our part with the engagements . . . of the treaty."[17] Informed as Hammond was about American handling of the Loyalists and the debts, he was unprepared to quote specific instances and turned to Bond for help. Bond was delighted.

Within a few days, he explained, he could present Hammond with obvious examples of American infractions! He had been gathering information since the beginning of his consulship. But given a little more time, he could do even better than that. He could arm Hammond with a list of state laws and acts, of executive orders and edicts, of court cases and judicial decisions that would stun the American secretary of state. Most of the infractions had occurred during the Confederate period, when Jefferson, as minister to France, was out of the country. He would never have heard of half of them. Bond could furnish such a substantial and comprehensive body of proof that the British memorial would preclude contradiction, and would end, once and for all, the cavil and the quibbling over the peace treaty. Hammond was enthusiastic. He thought it well worth the time Bond needed. Grenville's instructions had been very clear that Hammond was to consider American execution of the articles pertaining to the debts and the Loyalists "as the first and leading Object" of his mission.[18]

The minister and the consul went to work. For three months they collected information, arranged, codified, wrote, and rewrote. On March 5, 1792, Hammond sent the completed countermemorial to Jefferson. On the next day, he sent a copy to Grenville. In the accompanying note, he frankly admitted his pride in the enclosed manuscript and generously gave "Mr. Bond, His Majesty's Consul at this Place" full credit for the research and documentation.[19]

The British memorial was impressive in length, containing some eight thousand words of text and five appendixes.[20] Impressive, too, was the intricacy of the organization. Instead of treating first the Loyalists and then the debts owed the English and Scottish merchants, the paper handled the two subjects as woof and warp, weaving them into a complicated pattern.

The first indictment fell upon the United States Congress. An astute beginning, since it enabled the British to point out that the American government itself had confessed to infractions of the peace agreement in the circular letter of April 1787 in which congress regretted that "in some of the States, too little attention appears to have been paid to the public faith, pledged by the treaty." Congress—it was true—had recommended compliance but had failed to enforce it. Yet, suggested the paper, the peace negotiators would never have engaged congress to make recommendations "which they did not expect to be effectual."[21]

The states received the second charge for having enacted legislation during hostilities inimical to the Loyalists and the British creditors and for having failed after the war to repeal the acts. "A general repeal . . . would have been a compliance with the terms of the treaty." But in most states there was no restitution of the "estates, rights, and properties, of real British subjects" or of those who had resided in districts occupied by British troops, nor were the acts obstructing the recovery of the debts removed from the statute books.

The third accusation dealt with the enactment of laws subsequent to the peace in contravention of the treaty relating to the estates of Loyalists, to their persons, and to the debts: laws confirming confiscations and forfeitures, reaffirming proscriptions and attainders, expelling aliens, delaying the time for the commencement of suits, providing for the payment of debts by installments, compelling creditors to take debtors' land in settlement, and issuing new tender and valuation bills.

The final condemnation was against the courts. They had delayed justice, tantamount, claimed the memorial, to a denial of justice. They had disallowed wartime interest and in cases involving British subjects in general, their proceedings had been prejudicial and "repugnant."

Because of the above infractions the memorial claimed "the King, my master," had deemed it expedient to suspend compliance with the seventh article, namely the evacuation of the northwest posts, but, pointed out the document, mere suspension could never be equated with direct violation.[22]

Although the difficulty of the presentation, necessitating—as it did—several readings, contributed to the formidability of the memorial, the real thrust lay in the appendixes. They listed ninety-four acts, edicts, judicial decisions, and cases to support the general statements in the text. The American secretary of state had asked for "particular acts." Well, there they were . . . ninety-four of

them; "a body of proof," in Hammond's own words, "so complete
and substantial as to preclude the probability of cavil and contradiction."[23] The bibliography gave the title, the place, and the date
for each citation, but deliberately withheld further description—a
strategy historians have failed to appreciate and as a result they
have criticized the memorial for being a maze of generalizations
insufficiently documented.

The whole point was to put the reader on the defensive. Without a thorough knowledge of the charges and acts cited it would be
impossible to formulate an intelligent response. An abundance of
detail would have made it entirely too easy for Mr. Jefferson; it
would have presented him with a ready-made arsenal. Bond and
Hammond were counting on Jefferson's personal unfamiliarity
with the period under discussion. He had left the country on his
mission as minister to France in July 1784 and had only returned
at the end of October 1789. It had taken Mr. Bond five years to
collect the data. Let the American secretary of state try to track
down the indictments and the sources in a few months. He would
find it impossible. The British memorial would stand as the last on
the contravention of the peace treaty. A brilliant beginning for
Hammond's mission; for Bond's, a climactic end.

Nothing was heard from Jefferson until the end of March.
Then the following letter arrived addressed to Hammond:

Philadelphia, March 30, 1792

Sir:
   A constant course of business has as yet put it out of my power
to prepare an answer to your letter of the 5th instant. In the meantime I have been taking measure to procure copies of the several
acts therein complained of, that I might save you the trouble of
producing proofs of them. My endeavors have failed in the instances
below cited, of which, therefore, I am constrained to ask you to
furnish the documents . . . I beg you to be assured that I would not
have given you the trouble to produce any proofs which I could
have obtained myself; and I hope it will be considered as an evidence of this, that the list subjoined is only 13 out of 94 numbers
which your appendix specifies. Of all the rest I either have, or
expect copies in consequence of the measures I have taken.[24]

As Bond and Hammond had anticipated, Jefferson was having

trouble with the citations, and it was also clear he was furious over the omission of "proofs," as he called them. But that he only lacked thirteen must have given Bond and Hammond pause for thought. Perhaps they had underestimated their opponent. Still nothing could be gained by reversing their policy. Hammond waited a week before replying, rather stiffly, that "all the cases to which you have alluded . . . have been collected from the manuscript notes of a friend [i.e., Bond] and I have no doubt of their being accurately reported." With deference, the minister suggested that Jefferson might obtain the documents "on application to the courts of the States in which the actions were tried."[25] Of course, no proofs were enclosed.

April passed without further word from the American state department. May, on the other hand, brought Hammond a congratulatory letter from the British department for foreign affairs. Grenville wrote that he expected "the full and able Statement transmitted by you to Mr. Jefferson . . . must have made a very considerable Impression on the Minds of all those to whom it may have been communicated."[26]

Meanwhile, Bond prepared for the trip to England. The leave he had requested, immediately after Hammond's arrival, had been granted; he must, therefore, find someone to act as proconsul during his absence. With an eye on a promotion, Bond elected Edward Thornton, secretary of the British legation. Thornton's patron was none other than Under-Secretary of State Burges.[27] Bond also called on friends and relatives to learn what he might purchase for them while in London. He made careful notes of the law books Jasper Yates required to fill out his library in Lancaster, and of the jewelry, millinery, and material upon which the ladies had set their hearts.

Time for the passage neared. Still no word from Jefferson. It looked as though Bond might depart before the American answer arrived. But on the 29th of May, a messenger delivered a large package at the British embassy.

It was the American counter countermemorial. And it was six times the size of the British . . . it was a book. Bond found it a mass "of desultory and extensive discussion," filled with the sophisms so typical of politicians.[28] But nothing he said could detract from Jefferson's incredible accomplishment; he had collected transcripts, letters, depositions, and affidavits for every one of the ninety-four citations. The task, as Jefferson admitted himself, had been difficult and possibly could never have been brought off had it not been for one fact that Bond and Hammond apparently overlooked: Congress was in session.[29] Representatives and senators from every state were in Philadelphia. Through them Jefferson got the documents. Having once procured them, he made certain to include every one in his memorial and to make the most of each.

He analyzed the ninety-four citations individually and whenever possible left the impression that the British had misrepresented the issues. With the Harrison decision (see Chap. VII), for example, Jefferson claimed that recently the Maryland legislature had "liberally" and "voluntarily" passed an act enabling Harrison's relatives, who were British and, after all, aliens, to inherit the estate. He inferred that as a result the British had no basis for complaint and should never have cited the case in their memorial.[30]

This infuriated Bond. The British memorial, as he pointed out to Lord Grenville, had not cited the Harrison decision "for the Purpose of investigating the Rules and Principles of Alienage."[31] Instead, the memorial had referred to the case as one of several that had inspired doubts in the minds of the British creditors "of their competence to acquire or hold real property within the United States."[32] Jefferson, according to Bond, and not Hammond, was guilty of misrepresentation.

Regardless of what Bond said, the memorial was a diplomatic masterpiece. Instead of remaining on the defensive where the British had hoped to keep him, Jefferson seized the offensive. Making excellent use of Vattel, Wolf, and other international jurists, he swept away the argument about state laws enacted during hostilities on the grounds that they were lawful acts of war and hence "things out of question."[33] He then proceeded to demolish one-half of the British memorial with a lesson on word usage. Article V of the treaty read that "Congress shall earnestly recommend" that the states provide for the restitution of Loyalist estates, rights, and properties. That congress had done. Was it necessary, questioned

Jefferson, to explain to people who shared the same language the difference between "*enacting* a thing to be done, and *recommending* it to be done?" He made the distinction very clear and introduced overwhelming evidence that the peace negotiators had understood the difference as had members of the house of commons and members of the house of lords.[34] He next described how each state had amended or repealed laws that operated against the persons, rights, or properties of the Loyalists.

There remained the debts owed the British merchants. Although it was the most difficult question to defend, Jefferson again seized the offensive. He approached the problem obliquely through the northwest posts. They were, pointed out Jefferson, very small posts capable of being evacuated within a few days. The order to withdraw from New York, the principal supply center for the British armies, arrived in April 1783; evacuation was completed in November. But no order was sent to the officers in the northwest, and, claimed the American memorial, "No legitimate reason can be assigned why that order might not have been given as early . . . as the order to evacuate New York; and *all delay, after this, was in contravention of the treaty.*"[35]

The British, in other words, and not the Americans were the first to break the solemn international agreement. Having made that point, Jefferson was able to argue that the retention of the posts, cutting Americans off from the fur trade, coupled with the loss of slaves and the loss of trade to the West Indies, deprived the debtors of the means of payment.

All of which Bond insisted "amounted to nothing more nor less than a verbose admission of palpable Breaches, committed by the different States, against the solemn Stipulation of the Treaty of Peace."[36] Indeed, he had a point. But to what avail? It was now clear that Jefferson, unlike Jay, would never admit that Great Britain had more to complain of the United States than had the United States of Great Britain. Another British memorial would only lead to another American memorial, to further recrimination and contradiction, to precisely what Bond and Hammond had hoped to end.

As a result Bond left for England carrying Jefferson's memorial. Hammond waited for instructions from Grenville; and Jefferson fumed that "if every move and counter-move was to cross the Atlantic, it would be a long game indeed."[37]

Bond was in London by the end of June. Happy to be back, as he worded it, in "this blessed Country . . . under the best King and the best Constitution in the Universe."[38] He took rooms at No. 28 St. Albans Street, in Pall Mall, and then reported to Whitehall. There he enjoyed a triumph of sorts.

The under-secretaries welcomed him warmly and extended dinner invitations. The president of the Committee of Trade came around to thank Bond personally for the work he had done and invited him to visit at his house.[39] Lord Grenville was cordial although very busy. His marriage to Ann Pitt, sister of the last Lord of Camelford, was only a few weeks away and Grenville was trying to clear his desk before taking an extended leave of absence. Bond presented Jefferson's memorial, but Grenville then had no time to read the volume. He asked Bond to peruse it attentively for him and prepare an analysis for his use. His Lordship did not expect to return to the office until the end of the year; there was, therefore, no need for Bond to render the report immediately. In the meanwhile, he might himself take a real vacation. And he did.

Bond spent July shopping for friends, family, and self,[40] and then went visiting. In September, he was with George Hammond's family at Kirk Ella in Yorkshire; from there he went to the Erskines in Lancashire. But the worsening international situation cut short his holiday—as it did Grenville's. Under-Secretary Aust recalled Bond.[41] In October, he was in London. On the 12th, he delivered to Whitehall his "Observations . . . of the Counter Memorial of the American Secretary of State" and waited for further instructions.

Again Grenville was preoccupied with other matters. Across the Channel the situation was rapidly deteriorating. France had proclaimed herself a republic. Louis XVI was in prison. The French armies had defeated the Prussians at Valmy and had occupied Nice and Savoy. Early in November came news of the French victory at Jemappes and their conquest of the Austrian Netherlands. Were Holland next, England could no longer main-

tain neutrality. In December, the King in Council issued a proclamation offering bounties to all who volunteered for service in
His Majesty's navy. By mid-January, Grenville was convinced of
the inevitability of war. He asked Mr. Bond to report to Downing
Street—the new home of the foreign office—and not for the purpose of discussing Jefferson's memorial. Already, events had
forced that problem into the background. It was, in fact, to become
permanently shelved. Grenville never sent Hammond any instructions regarding the memorial. As a result, Jefferson—not Bond
and Hammond—wrote the last memorial on noncompliance with
the Anglo-American peace treaty.

Grenville sought Bond's advice on quite a different matter.
The Secretary explained that war with France appeared imminent,
and in view of this threat the navy must be enlarged. As Bond must
know, voluntary enlistments always fell short, compelling the admiralty to fall back upon the system of pressing sailors into service.
In previous correspondence, the consul had called attention to the
large number of British seamen navigating American vessels,[42] and
the foreign office must now define impressment policy with respect
to American bottoms. Should permission be given British commanders to board and search American ships and take off British
seamen? The practice would lead to strained relations with the
United States, whose government could be counted on to protest;
for it was inevitable that mistakes would occur and some Americans would be pressed into the British navy. American and British
sailors, after all, looked alike, talked alike, and acted alike. During
the Nootka Sound crisis, when war had threatened with Spain, the
press gangs had in error forced some Americans into service; and
at that time the United States had filed formal objections.[43] Therefore, would Mr. Bond study the matter and present a written report, as soon as possible, giving his opinions and suggestions.

For roughly a fortnight, Bond pondered over the question of
impressment and arrived at the conclusion that it was essentially an
economic problem. Bond reasoned that in the event of war the
United States, as a new and militarily weak country, would proclaim neutrality and that would mean "American Vessels must,
inevitably, become the Carriers, in a certain Degree of the Powers

at War." The degree, as Bond saw it, would depend upon impressment. America had the resources and knowledge with which to build ships, but lacked the men to sail them. Traditionally, Americans took to the land rather than the sea. This, Bond pointed out, explained why Yankee skippers offered such "extraordinary Wages," with the result that "even in a time of profound Peace, our Ships," wrote Bond, "are often deserted by the whole Crew, in the ports of the United States." With war, the desertions would increase; not only would it be profitable to sail under the stars and stripes, but it would also be safe. Then the United States would have the ships and the men. The war, in Bond's own words, "would operate most beneficially, in favor of the Navigation of that Country, & most fatally to the Navigation of this." If America seized the world's carrying trade, His Majesty's armies could be victorious on every battlefield, and still Great Britain would lose the war. Therefore, Bond concluded, there must be no relaxation "in the present mode of boarding American Vessels and pressing such Seamen, as are deemed British Subjects."

Since fraud could easily enter into the business of proving citizenship, Bond suggested that the British consuls in the United States issue certificates to *bona fide* American sailors. The consuls would base their declarations on church records or on the oaths of several "reputable" witnesses. The attestations would represent valid proof and protect the seamen.[44] Grenville accepted the suggestion and presented it to the American government. But the two nations were unable then or later to agree on a plan that was mutually satisfactory.[45]

In view of things to come it was altogether fitting that Bond finished the analysis and delivered it to Downing Street on February 1, 1793; on the day France declared war against Great Britain. For the duration of the titanic struggle the demands of the Royal Navy precluded any relaxation in the custom of pressing seamen into the service. For the next twenty years impressment plagued Anglo-American relations and proof of citizenship remained a burning issue between the two countries.

The official declaration of war reached London on the 8th of February. For Bond events then moved very quickly. Overnight the

British consular service in the United States assumed a new importance. On the 9th, the foreign office informed him he would henceforth receive £1,000 sterling per annum—top consular salary—and also would be reimbursed for any "extraordinary Travelling" performed in the line of duty.[46] On the 22nd, Bond had another long interview with Grenville. Together they reorganized the consular service in America.

Undoubtedly, Grenville would have liked to commission Bond consul general for all the United States, but Sir John Temple remained very much alive. Although his performance was at the best perfunctory, still he had given no real cause for recall. And so the Secretary of State compromised. He demoted Temple to consul general for the New England states and promoted Bond to consul general for the middle Atlantic and southern states.[47]

Next, came the filling of vacancies. From now on the British consuls in America must function as counterintelligence agents; it was, as a result, essential that every important American port be covered. Bond felt this would be accomplished were there consuls at Baltimore, Maryland, and Newport, Rhode Island. Grenville concurred and asked for candidates. Since for Bond the family always came first, he unhesitatingly recommended his uncle, Thomas William Moore, and in repayment for Burges' kindnesses, Edward Thornton. Grenville accepted the recommendations. It was agreed that Moore should serve as vice-consul at Newport, Thornton at Baltimore, and that both appointments were temporary, for the duration of the war only and that each would receive £300 a year.[48] Grenville arranged for Bond to pay both consuls and thus deprived poor Sir John of the privilege of paying an officer in his own area.

The interview ended with Grenville's request that Bond return to America at once. Immediately Bond found out about sailings. Learning that several vessels were about to leave for the United States, he hurriedly packed; he submitted his final reports to the foreign office; he picked up instructions for Hammond and for Temple; he left London and overtook a ship at Bristol.

On the 5th of May, after a thirty-eight day passage, Bond was in Philadelphia. This time when he submitted his credentials there was no difficulty. "It is with great Satisfaction," he was able to write Grenville, "that my Commission as his Majesty's Consul General for the Middle and Southern States of America was, immediately, recognized upon my Arrival here, by the President of the United States, and that I have already entered upon the Duties of my office, to which I beg your Lordship to believe I shall pay the most unremitting Attention."[49] And, of course, he did.

NOTES

[1] Although born in Philadelphia, Robert Barclay lived, for most of his life, in England where he had large business interests, among them the Southwark brewery in Southwark. For Nash & Martin Co. see CAD COLL, PB, "Neate Misc." Box; for the Erskine letter to Bond, Sargeants Inn, January 31, 1791, "I-K" Box.

[2] Soon after his arrival John Travis joined the Society of the Sons of St. George—something Bond never did although his father and uncle were founding members. In time, Travis became the society's treasurer and one of the ruling Committee of Eight. He also was manager of the Philadelphia Assembly. In short, he was socially as well as monetarily acceptable; by courtesy of Francis James Dallett, former librarian of the Athenaeum of Philadelphia; Theodore C. Knaff, *A History of the Society of the Sons of St. George, Established at Philadelphia for the Advice and Assistance of Englishmen in Distress* (Philadelphia, 1923); Christ Church Records, Marriages.

[3] Bond to Leeds, Philadelphia, January 3, 1790, *AHAAR*, 1897, 454–455. For a description of the interview see Col. John Hamilton to Leeds, Norfolk, April 10, 1791, and Bond to Leeds, Philadelphia, April 12, 1791, FO 4/9.

[4] Bond to Burges, Philadelphia, April 12, 1791, Burges Papers, Bodleian Library, Oxford University, Oxford, England.

[5] Bond to Grenville, Philadelphia, August 2, 1791, *AHAAR*, 1897, 485.

[6] Until Frazer retired, there was only a single under-secretary of state for the foreign department; after that there were two.

[7] Burges to Bond, Whitehall, August 3, 1791, Burges Papers.

[8] Secretary of State Carnarvon to George III and Mrs. Williamina Cadwalader to her sister, quoted by Beckles Willson, *Friendly Relations, A Narrative of Britain's ministers and Ambassadors to America, 1791–1930* (Boston, 1934), pp. 4, 6.

[9] Quoted by D. B. Horn, *The British Diplomatic Service, 1689–1789* (Oxford, 1961), p. 256.

[10] Temple to Leeds, New York, September 2, 1790, April 21, 1791, Henry Adams Transcripts, Library of Congress. Anticipating that Sir John would move to Philadelphia, Bond wrote for instructions as to his "future Disposal and Residence." See Bond to Leeds, Philadelphia, August 2, 1790, FO 4/8; September 1, 1790, *AHAAR*, 1897, 461.

[11] Bond to Grenville, Philadelphia, November 25, 1791, *AHAAR*, 1897, 494. Bond had requested a leave in the fall of 1789, after he made up his mind to take on private practice, but Whitehall turned it down because of the study of America that the Lords of Trade had just undertaken. See Chap. VII.

[12] This was in accordance with instructions from Grenville to Bond, Whitehall, September 1791, FO 4/11.

[13]Bond to Grenville, Philadelphia, November 1, 1791, FO 4/5.

[14]Quoted by Willson, *Friendly Relations,* p. 6 and by Leslie Reade, "George III to the United States Sendeth Greetings. . . ." *History Today VIII* (November 1958), 770.

[15]Burges to Bond, Whitehall, January 3, 1792, Burges Papers.

[16]Hammond to Grenville, Philadelphia, December 6, 1791, February 2, 1792, October 3, 1792, *Instructions to the British Ministers to the United States, 1791–1812,* Bernard Mayo, ed. (Washington, D.C., 1941), p. 81.

[17]Jefferson to Hammond, Philadelphia, December 15, 1791, *American State Papers, Foreign Relations* (Washington, D.C., 1832), I, 190.

[18]See Grenville to Hammond, Whitehall, September 2, 1791, *Instructions to the British Ministers,* p. 14.

[19]*Instructions to the British Ministers,* p. 24.

[20]For the text of the British memorial see *ASP,FR,* I, 193–200; for the best account—albeit from the American point of view—of the battle of the memorials see Samuel F. Bemis, *Jay's Treaty, A Study in Commerce and Diplomacy,* (New York, 1924) pp. 95–108 and Dumas Malone, *Jefferson and the Rights of Man* (Boston, 1951), pp. 412–419.

[21]*ASP,FR,* I, 194.

[22]*ASP,FR,* I, 197.

[23]*Instructions to the British Ministers,* p. 24.

[24]*ASP,FR,* I, 200.

[25]Hammond to Jefferson, Philadelphia, April 6, 1792, *ASP,FR,* I, 200.

[26]Grenville to Hammond, Whitehall, April 25, 1792, *Instructions to the British Ministers,* p. 24.

[27]Thornton had tutored Burges' sons. The Under-Secretary placed him as Hammond's secretary and wrote to Bond that Mr. Thornton, "a young Gentleman . . . for whom I have a particular regard, and in whose welfare I greatly interest myself, I beg leave therefore to recommend . . . to your acquaintance, and shall thank you for any attention or assistance you may think proper to afford him." Burges to Bond, Whitehall, August 3, 1791, Burges Papers. See also the unpublished memoirs of Sir Edward Thornton, Manuscript Division, Library of Congress.

[28]Bond to Grenville, St. Albans Street, October 12, 1792, *AHAAR,* 1897, 500.

[29]See Notes of a Conversation with Hammond, June 3, 1792, Thomas Jefferson, *The Complete Anas of Thomas Jefferson,* Franklin B. Sawvel, ed. (New York, 1903), p. 76.

[30]*ASP,FR,* I, 196.

[31]Bond to Grenville, St. Albans Street, October 12, 1792, *AHAAR,* 1897, 512.

[32]*ASP,FR,* I, 196.

[33]*ASP,FR,* I, 201.

[34]*ASP,FR,* I, 202–203.

[35]*ASP,FR,* I, 207.

[36]Bond to Grenville, St. Albans Street, October 12, 1792, *AHAAR,* 1897, 500.

[37]*Anas of Thomas Jefferson,* p. 77.

[38]Bond to Jasper Yates, London, July 15, 1792, Gratz Collection, HSP.

[39]See Bond's "thank-you letter" to Lord Hawkesbury, Bristol, March 15, 1793, Liverpool Papers, Official Correspondence, PRO, Add. Ms. 38/228.

[40]See Bond to Yates, London, July 1792; Yates to Bond, Lancaster, September 1792, Yates Collection, HSP. Also see vouchers for clothes from H. Fisher &

Son; for jewelry and silver from Wm. Moore, Ludgate Street; for a pair of steel spectacles and case, –10–, from P. J. Dollon, North side of St. Paul's Church Yard, CAD COLL, PB, "Voucher" Box.

[41]Bond to Aust, Kirkella, September 20, 1792, *AHAAR,* 1897, 498.

[42]See, for instance, Bond to Leeds, Philadelphia, September 18, 1790, *AHAAR,* 1897, 462.

[43]Gouverneur Morris, who was then in London, filed the official protests of the United States government with the Duke of Leeds, making the comment that "I believe, my Lord, this is the only instance in which we are not treated as aliens." See Morris to George Washington, London, May 29, 1790, *ASP,FR,* I, 124.

[44]Bond to Grenville, St. Albans Street, February 1, 1793, *AHAAR,* 1897, 524–527.

[45]See James Fulton Zimmerman, *Impressment of American Seamen* (New York, 1925) pp. 44–45.

[46]See Bond's formal application, February 9, 1793, FO 5/2.

[47]Grenville to Hammond, Downing Street, March 8, 1793, *Instructions to British Ministers,* p. 36. The Committee of London Merchants at a meeting on July 25, 1792 composed a memorial requesting wider powers for Mr. Bond, which Grenville received on August 3, 1792, FO 4/16.

[48]Bond to Grenville, St. Albans Street, February 23, 1793; Downing Street, March 12, 1793, FO 5/2.

[49]Bond to Grenville, Philadelphia, May 17, 1793, *AHAAR,* 1897, 527.

CHAPTER NINE

The Consul in Wartime

Philadelphia, in the spring of 1793, was a different city from the one Bond had left the year before. Not that it had changed in appearance; the streets and buildings were the same; Bond thought the capital was still the airiest, cleanest, neatest, modern city in the world.[1] But the people had changed. They seemed to Bond deranged, as though in the grips of a strange fever that produced even in the most level-headed of its victims a mad, unreasoning love for everything French.

Bond had been on the high seas—taking his daily constitutionals around the deck of the packet, *Birmingham*—when the French fever first struck Philadelphia. During the last week of March, vessels coming into port brought word that France and England were at war. The fever started. During the next weeks, the unofficial reports increased. Then in the middle of May came official confirmation. It was really true: America's "first and best Ally" was at war with the tyrant king, George III![2]

President Washington hurried to the capital from Mt. Vernon. The cabinet met in emergency sessions. On the 22nd of April, the United States government issued—what Bond and Grenville had anticipated—a proclamation of neutrality. But for months it remained doubtful whether that document would amount to more than a piece of paper. Treaties of alliance and commerce tied the American government to France, while American public opinion remained far from neutral. In Philadelphia enthusiasm for the French kept mounting; Anglophobia intensified; and general frenzy gripped the city.

Rumors were everywhere. Any bit of foreign news was seized upon, repeated, enlarged, and distorted beyond recognition. Toward the end of April, a report began to circulate that a British official was on his way to the United States—as, indeed, Bond was. But after the street-corner politicians digested this intelligence, the official became none other than Guy Carleton, Lord Dorchester, and he was coming to Philadelphia as the new British ambassador. Americans loathed the very name, Dorchester. As governor-general of Canada, they held him primarily responsible for Britain's retention of the posts and for the arming of the Indians. The "Dorchester story" spread through the city, enflaming anti-British sentiment to such an extent that George Hammond became alarmed and tried through the press to quash it.[3] But the rumor persisted. It died only when the "official" appeared and when, instead of Lord Dorchester, he turned out to be plain old Phineas Bond back as consul general.

Bond arrived on Sunday, May the 5th. Bells rang, but they were for church. There was no crowd to greet him; no one cheered until his throat was hoarse; no guns fired in salute. Not that Bond expected any kind of demonstration. But eleven days later another foreign official entered the city. The welcome he received brought home to Bond the changes that had taken place in Philadelphia. What he heard and saw on that day made him realize how different and difficult his work was going to be now there was war.

The foreign official was the new minister from France, Edmund Genêt. Traveling overland from Charleston, South Carolina, he was expected to reach Philadelphia on May 16th. That morning, shortly after sunrise, the crowds began to gather in center city. The French frigate, *L'Embuscade*, slipped down river. When the crow's nest sighted Genêt's party nearing Grey's Ferry, the ship fired three of her thirty-four guns. That was the signal. At once every church bell began to peal; the crowds began to cheer; and thousands marched toward the ferry to meet Genêt and escort him into the capital.[4]

On the following day at the State House, a more formal celebration took place. The various Republican clubs and the Committee of Philadelphians, organized for the sole purpose of welcoming the minister, presented addresses. When the speeches ended, the civic leaders and "an immense body of citizens walking three abreast" led Genêt to the Century Tavern for refreshments. There toasts were drunk to him and to "Free France;" there hundreds of Philadelphians, whom Bond formerly considered "respectable," sang the Marseillaise.[5]

Nor did that end the entertainments. One dinner in honor of Genêt followed another with the press reporting each affair in detail. Bond was obliged to learn how many toasts to France had been made on the previous evening, how many stanzas of the Marseillaise had been sung, how many guests had donned the red-white-and-blue cockade, and how many times *L'Embuscade* had fired her guns. This enthusiasm for Britain's hereditary enemy was almost more than Bond could bear. Yet there was very little he could do about it.

He worried over the problem. He reached the conclusion that in time the French frenzy might be mitigated provided every Briton in Philadelphia conducted himself with the utmost probity and thereby placed himself above reproach. Hammond agreed; and both minister and consul general were extremely careful about their personal conduct. But it was up to Bond, not Hammond, to persuade other Englishmen to follow suit.

During May, Bond visited and talked with the British merchants, factors, and shipowners in the city. He found them, for the most part, cooperative and understanding. But another group of nationals proved less accessible and far less open to reason: the sailors off His Britannic Majesty's merchant vessels.

Bond could hardly expect that a British seaman, especially after a few drinks in a Front Street tavern, would just keep on walking when he saw a French sailor. In honor of king and country he must knock that "damned . . . National Cockade" off the Frenchman's head, with the result that night after night brawls erupted along the waterfront. Bond spent a fair part of each day investigating the fracas of the previous evening. Neither his efforts nor the passing of time improved the situation. By the end of May, bands of French and British seamen, armed with cutlasses and clubs, ranged the city looking for one another.[6] Even in daytime the streets were no longer safe. Philadelphians demanded additional police protection.[7] Attacks on Great Britain increased in number and in vehemence.

The press represented the French sailors as the innocent victims and the British as the brutal perpetrators of every "Outrage." "Evening before last," read a typical account, "a French sailor was walking peaceably along Front Street . . . when he ran into four English sailors who knocked him down. . . ." Or according to another story, a group of British sailors encountered three French sailors walking in the street. The British informed them they were Americans, their friends, and offered to shake hands. The French accepted with pleasure . . . and the British beat them up.[8]

To try and set the record straight in cases where British sailors had been unjustly maligned, Bond called on Mayor Mathew Clarkson. The visit accomplished nothing; for Clarkson, as Bond reported to Grenville, was in favor of the French. As a last resort, Bond went to press. On the 31st of May, he placed the following announcement in every Philadelphia newspaper:

> His Britannic majesty's consul general for the middle and southern states of America, anxious to manifest his regard for the public peace of this city, and his respect for the laws & constitution of the United States, recommends, most earnestly, to the British seamen in the port of Philadelphia, and to all others, his majesty's subjects, to conduct themselves with the greatest moderation & good order.[9]

Some sailors probably took the plea to heart; by the second week of June, accounts of the riots dropped from the papers. But other factors helped ease the situation. The city fathers increased the police force in the Northern Liberties, the Moyamensing, and the Southwark sections of the city.[10] Then, on the 3rd of June, the chief cause of the disturbances removed itself; *L'Embuscade* weighed anchor and left port, reducing the number of French sailors at liberty in Philadelphia. The behavior of the British seamen improved. Peace returned to the city.

Nonetheless, the French frigate continued to present Bond with problems. She had on board twenty-one British prisoners of war, whom as Bond interpreted consular duties, he must try to liberate. He knew in the past powers at war had redeemed prisoners while hostilities were going on. Either they paid ransom, as

Britain had done in the last war with France, or they exchanged prisoners on the basis of a man for a man, a grade for a grade, and a rank for a rank. But these redemptions had only occurred after the belligerents first worked out the terms and conditions in a cartel or treaty.[11] As far as Bond knew in the current war no such agreement existed—and, in fact, there was none until 1798— which meant opening negotiations without the backing of authority.

Further disadvantages weakened his position. In the spring of 1793, there were no French prisoners in the vicinity of Philadelphia. Thus Bond had nothing to offer in exchange for the twenty-one Britons confined on *L'Embuscade,* for he was determined not to pay ransom. Recalling former experiences with the treasury lords, he foresaw the possibility of never being reimbursed. He was himself quite unprepared to bear the expense. Then, too, it was a matter of principle with him never to abet the enemy's war effort by providing him with financial aid.

Without any bargaining power, Bond opened negotiations with Monsieur Francois DuPont, the French consul at Philadelphia. Somewhat to Bond's surprise he found DuPont a pleasant, reasonable man of the world. The French consul admitted that, although the British at the moment had no prisoners, the day would undoubtedly dawn when the situation would be otherwise. Then Mr. Bond, whose word he trusted, could equalize the exchange. DuPont, in short, accepted Bond's I.O.U. and promised to arrange matters with Jean Baptiste Francois Bompart, Captain of *L'Embuscade.*[12]

A few days later, the French consul informed the British consul that Captain Bompart had agreed to release the prisoners in two groups. DuPont requested receipts. Bond, in no position to challenge the Frenchman's word by refusing to make out the certificates, signed for two masters, three mates, one ship's carpenter, a boatswain, and fourteen seamen and solemnly pledged that "I do hereby promise and engage that an equal Number of french Prisoners, in a similar Capacity, shall be restored to france."[13]

Before *L'Embuscade* sailed Captain Bompart released seventeen of the British prisoners. But there had been a misunderstanding. The frigate left Philadelphia with four British seamen still on board. According to Bond, Bompart needed the men to sail the ship and God alone knew when those four would be liberated. Yet there existed an attestation above the signature of P. Bond that the seamen had been released. For more than a month Bond fretted over the possible repercussions of his error. Then a letter arrived from Sir John Temple; a French frigate, *L'Embuscade,* had anchored in New York harbor and a Captain Bompart had handed to Temple four British seamen!

Thus Bond's first negotiation over prisoners of war ended satisfactorily. Of greater significance was the precedent Bond and DuPont had established. For the duration of the war—and quite contrary to twentieth-century practice—French and British consuls in the United States exchanged prisoners in an atmosphere of relative amiability and on the basis of a seaman for a seaman, a soldier for a soldier, and a rank for a rank. Ransom, that ancient means of redeeming captives, never entered the picture. Moreover, when France and Britain finally negotiated a treaty for the exchange of prisoners in 1798, there were no provisions for ransom; the basis of exchange was the same as that set up by Bond and DuPont.[14]

In order to redeem British prisoners, Bond maintained polite relations with the French officials at Philadelphia. But at the same time he did everything in his power to foil their operations and to bring about the destruction of their country. When he first opened negotiations with Monsieur DuPont, his career as a British secret agent had already begun.

It seemed a strange role for a man like Bond who placed such stress on social conventions and proprieties. Yet this was a man who delighted in sporting wildly colored waistcoats and who was never happier than when he was sitting in a stall at the theater. Beneath the fastidious exterior, lurked a flair for the dramatic. Bond had curbed the bent for forty-three years; now, in the line of duty, he might loosen the reins. With enormous enthusiasm he became a spy.

While he engaged in civilities with DuPont, Bond sent messages about *L'Embuscade* to the commanders of the British naval stations at Halifax, Jamaica, and Antigua. The dispatches described the frigate's size and strength and the danger she presented to British shipping. In the letters to the Caribbean, Bond suggested that the frigate's destination might be Santo Domingo. In the report to Halifax, he expressed the hope that a British warship might be spared and sent south to intercept *L'Embuscade* when she left Delaware Bay.[15]

Although he had notified all British naval stations in the western hemisphere, Bond felt still more could be done. There was an outside chance that some of His Majesty's ships of war might be cruising along the United States coast. If he could get word to them, they would be in the best position to catch *L'Embuscade*. It meant hiring a boat to go in search; and that involved money. He laid the plan before Hammond. When he received the minister's approbation, Bond went ahead and engaged a pilot boat to cruise between the Virginia Capes and Long Island.

The experiment cost ninety dollars and it failed.[16] In the spring of 1793, there simply were no British warships off the American coast. At the beginning of the war, the West Indian stations had only two 50-gun ships and a half dozen small frigates and sloops. At Halifax there was a single 64-gun ship-of-the-line, three small frigates, and four small sloops.[17] For months to come, naval supremacy in American waters belonged to the French.

Nonetheless, from Halifax sailed the *Boston,* a 32-gun frigate, under the command of George William Augustus Courtenay, with instructions to intercept and capture the 34-gun *L'Embuscade*. The *Boston* engaged *L'Embuscade* early in the morning of August 1st off Sandy Hook. Both were frigates, mounting almost the same number of guns, but the French ship was by far the heavier. She displaced nine hundred and six tons to the *Boston*'s six hundred and seventy-six. Furthermore, Captain Bompart outfought and outsailed Captain Courtenay. Within an hour the *Boston*'s main topmast and mizzen mast were down; the jib and foresail were shot away, and the gaff destroyed. At twenty minutes past six a single cannon ball from *L'Embuscade* killed both Captain Courtenay and the commanding officer of the marines. The *Boston* then put before the wind and managed to escape. Victoriously, *L'Embuscade* sailed into New York harbor to the joy of the inhabitants, who immediately fell victim to the French fever.[18]

Bond could flatter himself that he had brought about the first naval engagement of the war in American waters. That it terminated in a British defeat bitterly disappointed him. But as reports arrived from New York to the effect that all *L'Embuscade*'s masts must be taken out for repairs, Bond's spirits rose. At least for a few weeks the French frigate would be unable to prey upon British merchantmen.

There remained the French privateers. Carrying between four to six guns, these small vessels hid in harbors up and down the American coast; then, as British carriers neared land, they would dart forth to seize them. Bond had barely caught his breath after the long journey from England before he must face the problem of the privateers.

At four o'clock in the afternoon of May the 3rd—two days before Bond reached Philadelphia—the *William* of Glasgow, forty-two days out of Bremen and bound for Maryland, was off the Cape Henry light. The pilot had been on board an hour. He was taking the vessel into the mouth of the Chesapeake with a leading wind, when suddenly, as he later said, "a small schooner came in sight, coming out from the capes." She ran alongside, fired one gun, commanded the *William* to haul down her colors and to heave to the eastward. The schooner was the French privateer, *Citizen Genêt*. She put out a small boat. A lieutenant and six men boarded the *William*, took possession of the ship, and removed the master and most of the hands—they became prisoners of war and were among those whom Bond later liberated from *L'Embuscade*. On May 11th, the *William* was in Philadelphia. There, acting as an admiralty court, Consul DuPont officially condemned her as a prize of war and prepared for an auction sale of the vessel and the cargo.[19]

Immediately the owners of the *William* called on Bond. There were seven; all British citizens; all at the moment in Philadelphia.[20] Naturally, they wanted their ship and expected Bond to bring about its restitution.

He investigated. He found out no appeal could be lodged with Secretary of State Jefferson until the legal "Modes of Redress" had been exhausted. He took into account the American public's pro-French proclivities and the resulting necessity for Englishmen in the United States to act with circumspection. Above all, he brought his legal knowledge to bear upon the problem. He reached the conclusion that the owners had a strong case and ought, therefore, to enter suit in the federal district court.

As Bond saw it, the Fench minister had commissioned and equipped the *Citizen Genêt* in Charleston, South Carolina, after the United States had proclaimed neutrality, but before he had himself presented his credentials to the President. As a result, according to Bond, "Considerable Doubts" existed as to the authenticity of the commission and as to the legality of the privateer. Also, the case involved the "interesting" question whether *"at any Time"* belligerents might legally fit out privateers in the ports of a neutral country. The court, in Bond's opinion, would consider these practices "as direct Insults, offered to the Rights of Sovereignty of the United States," in which event not only would the seizure of the *William* be deemed illegal but the case would set a far-reaching precedent.[21]

Bond was always practical; so he advised the owners to emphasize that the seizure had occurred in neutral waters. According to the master, James Legget, the *William* was two or at the most two and a half miles off Cape Henry when taken. Bond realized that the United States government had still to define its territorial limits, but he banked on the fact that three miles from shore—or the utmost distance covered by a cannon shot—represented the shortest limits claimed by any nation in the world. On that point alone, it was Bond's conviction, the court would rule in favor of restitution.[22]

He miscalculated. He was trying to reason out the moves in a game for which there were no rules. Nothing developed as he thought it would.

At the end of June, the case came before the federal district court in Philadelphia. Judge Peters ruled that "the Ship or Property taken as Prize . . . does not pertain to the Court" and is a matter for the executive rather than the judicial branch of government. He dismissed the libel.[23]

That was a blow Bond had failed to foresee. Although different from what Bond had anticipated, the decision set a precedent. District court after district court followed Peters's lead and refused to act in prize cases, with the result that Hammond was obliged to negotiate each one separately with Jefferson.

The affair of the *William* dragged on. Bond's deductions were proved correct in only one instance. The case did force the United States to establish its territorial jurisdiction. At the end of the year, Jefferson proclaimed the three-mile limit. But by then the evidence had blurred. It appeared that when taken the *William* was farther from land than her master had suggested, and that she had been beyond the three-mile belt. The unexpected development taught Bond "that nothing can be more fallacious than distances at Sea." That lesson he never forgot.[24]

The dispute over the *William* was finally settled in 1798. The joint commission established under article seven of Jay's treaty reviewed the appeal of the owners. All the points Bond had raised were ignored. Instead, the judges ruled that prior to June 5, 1793, when the United States ordered the departure of privateers equipped in American ports, those privateers were legal instruments of war and their seizures represented the legitimate spoils of war. Again, the case was dismissed.[25]

But the *William* was only the beginning. Prize cases broke thick and fast during the spring and summer of 1793. There was the *Fanny* and the *Active* of Bermuda; there was the *Catherine* and the *Little Sarah*. There were so many that Bond and Hammond made little attempt to define what part of the business the consul ought to handle and what part belonged to the minister. They shared the work. While Bond, for instance, coped with the *William,* Hammond saw the *Fanny* through the courts.

This cooperation would never have been possible had the minister disliked the consul general. As it was, the two men were on even more intimate terms than before. Unwittingly, Bond had made Hammond a very happy man. When the minister first arrived, Bond had introduced him to his lifelong friend, Andrew Allen, and to the Allen family. While Bond was on leave, Hammond and the eldest daughter, Margaret, fell in love. They waited until Bond returned from England. Then, on May 20, 1793, at Christ's Church, George Hammond and Margaret Allen were married.[26] For the second time, Bond had proved his prowess as a matchmaker and in the process had become a true friend of George Hammond.

The minister so trusted the consul that he permitted him to function even on the diplomatic level. For instance, and contrary to what historians have thought, it was Bond rather than Hammond who terminated the affair of the *Jane*.[27]

That case presented the other side of the privateer question; for the *Jane* was a British armed vessel. She entered the Philadelphia port early in July and proceeded to cut new portholes and mount additional guns and carriages. At the end of the month, Secretary of War Henry Knox sent a note to Hammond, pointing out "that no Augmentation of Force of Vessels belonging to any of the belligerent Powers, can be permitted in our Ports." Knox ordered Hammond to see that the *Jane* reduced "her Force to the Situation it was at the Time of her Arrival."[28] Just then Hammond was preparing to go to New York. He found it inconvenient to enter into negotiations and so asked Bond to take care of the matter.

Bond went on board the *Jane*. He talked to the captain and to the owners. He watched the custom officials survey the vessel. They found the *Jane* had augmented her force—as, indeed, she had. But in Bond's mind there was a vast difference between the fitting out of a French ship and the mounting of a few guns on a British vessel. The *Jane*, as Bond explained to Knox, was not a privateer. She was a merchantman armed in self-defense and would never cruise or engage "in offensive Attacks upon an Enemy." Bond even tried to excuse the additional guns. His letter to Knox read in part:

> The owners of the Ship Jane . . . have not added a single Gun to the Number they brought with them—nor have they made any Alteration in Point of Force unless the Substitution from new, instead of old Gun Carriages can be so considered:— . . . the old Waistboards, which are still to be seen, were pierced for Guns precisely in the same Manner as the new ones are . . . the two port Holes in the Stern are in the Place of two Venetian Windows which the Ship had when she had a round House, & which then could have been used as port Holes.[29]

Knox would have none of it. On the same day, he shot back an emphatic order for Bond to reduce the *Jane*'s force.[30] Bond acqui-esced. The portholes were closed, the four new gun carriages put ashore, the additional guns dismounted, and the *Jane* sailed.

Two weeks before the French minister, Genêt, in a similar situ-ation disobeyed the orders of the American government and per-mitted the privateer, *La Petite Démocrate,* to sail. Bond might have done the same. But he submitted in order to demonstrate that the British were far more reasonable and law-abiding than the French. It proved an astute move. The affair of *La Petite Démocrate* cost Genêt his commission. Had Bond let the *Jane* sail without disman-tling, he would have lost his exequatur.

In submitting, Bond had taken public opinion into account. The very presence of the *Jane*—the only armed British ship in Philadelphia—had given the pro-French faction an opportunity to renew their attacks on the British. It would, Bond thought, have been foolish for him to add coals to the fire.

In spite of the *Jane*'s departure and Bond's almost exemplary handling of the affair, anti-British sentiment continued to rise. From Norfolk, Virginia, it looked to Consul Hamilton as though revolution were going to break out in Philadelphia "from the feuds of the Violent and Moderate Parties." The crisis so frightened him, he asked Lord Grenville for "discretionary Power . . . to return home whenever the Urgency of the Occasion may justify such a Step."[31]

Bond, who was in the midst of the furor, never even sent a dispatch about it. He was too busy tracking the maneuvers of a large French fleet that had arrived from Santo Domingo. He alerted Halifax that troops were being provided "with coarse thick cloth Uniforms," which suggested an attack on the British fisheries. His reports listing the French ships at New York, in the Chesapeake, and in the Delaware poured into the admiralty.[32]

Bond was too occupied to pay attention to the tolling of the church bells and to the increasing number of funeral processions passing through the streets. As he later said, it had been "an un-commonly intemperate Summer,"[33] and the amount of sickness failed to surprise him. But, by the third week in August, there was hardly a family in Philadelphia that was free of illness. Fires burned at every street corner to purge the air. Mayor Clarkson stopped the tolling of the bells and ordered all houses with sickness marked.[34] Hammond's household was disrupted; four servants there were ill. Dr. Benjamin Rush treated them with "strong but safe mercurial purges." They appeared to recover. Then a few weeks later two died.[35] The yellow fever had struck Philadelphia. Still Bond stayed in the city.

In the second week of September, it seemed to one physician, as though the disease had awakened, "like a giant refreshed by wine."[36] It was then Bond became frightened. Together with his mother and sisters he fled to the family estate in Chester County, Moore Hall.[37] There they remained in good health, while Bond enjoyed the respite from work; for, as he might have said, it had been "an uncommonly busy Summer."

Bond and his immediate family were fortunate. Over four thousand Philadelphians, or roughly ten per cent of the population, died that year from the fever. The toll left Bond with a horror of the plague that he never overcame.

Early in November, the weather turned cold; there was a succession of frosts, and the fever abated. Bond remained in the country. He had become convinced the oppressive, muggy, four-month heat spell, although it might not have caused the epidemic, accounted for the rapidity with which the disease had spread. He, therefore, insisted "the Air must undergo, not only a complete, but a continued, unremitted Change." Even after that, he foresaw danger from careless people who might not properly disinfect their houses and might expose "the Apparel and Bedding of the Sick."[38]

At the end of the month, the city appeared safe. Bond sent several servants ahead to cleanse the new house he had bought just before the outbreak of the epidemic. Realizing he would be in Philadelphia for the duration of the war and having always considered the Union Street house as too small and unpretentious, he found himself for the second time establishing a suitable consulate.

The new house was on the north side of Chestnut Street between Fifth and Sixth Streets and opposite the State House. It was an elegant, three-story, red-brick dwelling, with two trees by the front door that raised the insurance premiums but set Phineas

Bond's messuage apart from other houses in the block. In the rear was a piazza, where the consul might entertain guests on a summer evening; in the basement was a huge, thirty-three by fifteen-foot kitchen.[39]

Bond's mother sold the Union Street house at a profit, and at once she and his sisters, Frances and Rebecca, moved to the consulate to look after Phineas. By the beginning of 1794, the new household was running smoothly and Bond was back at work.

Unfortunately, the situation had never been more critical. The pro-French faction had ceased to represent merely a section of public opinion and had instead become a political party with formidable strength in both houses of congress. The third congressional session had opened. Once again the house of representatives was debating the placement of discriminatory duties against England. This time, because of the pro-French or Republican party, Bond feared the bill would pass. Congressmen who had hitherto been noted for their moderation were making acrimonious attacks on Great Britain. Their speeches aired the old complaints: Britain's retention of the northwest posts; the Indian wars; "and to these," wrote Bond, "is now superadded the suspension of Hostilities between Portugal and Algiers, which is imputed to the Interposition of Great Britain, and ascribed to our Desire," to let loose the Barbary pirates on American shipping and thus "to effectually destroy the Commerce of the United States." Whether America will continue neutral, Bond wrote Grenville, or will enter the war on the side of France "is at this Moment, a very questionable Point."[40] Indeed, it was.

In March 1794, reports reached Philadelphia that over two hundred and fifty American vessels had been seized in the West Indies and carried into British ports for prize-court adjudication. The seizures were in accordance with a British order-in-council designed to hurt France by stopping neutral trade with the French islands.[41] But this news on top of other grievances caused the American public to clamor for war.

No Englishman, walking the streets of any coastal town, escaped insults, and what Bond referred to as "indecent Threats." The British minister and the consul endured their full share of name calling. But Philadelphians had menaced Bond before; he met the rebukes with, as he put it, "a very cool Indifference."[42]

Although confident he could take care of himself, he remained uneasy about other British consuls. Americans in the south appeared more prone than the inhabitants of the capital to take the law into their own hands. And, as consul general, Bond was responsible for the safety of the men in his command. He, therefore, kept a close watch on conditions in Virginia and Maryland.

At Norfolk, Consul John Hamilton faced a series of unpleasantnesses. The first occurred when he entertained a visiting Englishman by taking him to dinner and the theater. At the end of the performance, to Hamilton's horror, the "young Gentleman" called in a loud voice for *"an old English Song."* Hamilton managed to get the traveler out of the theater and out of Norfolk that night. A very good thing it was, for the next day a lynching mob was outside the consulate demanding that Hamilton hand over the Englishman to them.[43]

No sooner had the town quieted down over the old-English-song episode than the British frigate, *Daedalus,* sailed into port. She was a store ship, under the command of Sir Charles Knowles, and had put in for refitting and provisions. As in the case of the *Jane,* the presence of the only armed British vessel in the port caused tempers to flare. In addition to which, an American sea captain at Norfolk spread the story that the *Daedalus* had impressed two of his hands and had fired at his ship, killing a horse. The alleged outrages whipped the citizens into a frenzy. They formed a mob and armed with torches marched to the docks where they set the *Daedalus* on fire. She narrowly escaped total destruction.[44]

Hamilton managed to settle the affair. He convinced the Virginians that no horse had been shot and no men impressed. One seaman had voluntarily signed on the *Daedalus.* But to calm tempers and to abide by Bond's instructions concerning British behavior in the United States, Hamilton and Sir Charles obtained another hand for the American captain as a replacement for the sailor who had come on the *Daedalus.* Bond was pleased with the manner in which the consul and Sir Charles had conducted themselves. In Bond's estimation, both were capable of handling the difficult situation in Norfolk.[45]

But Thornton in Baltimore was young, without Hamilton's years of experience and without the protection of the *Daedalus'* thirty-two guns. And he was under constant attack. The news had just reached Baltimore that Captain Joshua Barney, one of the town's most beloved characters, was in prison at Kingston, Jamaica, awaiting trial for assault and battery. When the British seized Barney's vessel, he had—like the good Marylander he was—put up a fight and seriously injured the prize-master and several British seamen. Bond was afraid of what might happen if the court convicted and punished Barney; the Baltimoreans might take vengeance upon Thornton. The consul general preferred not to wait and see. He ordered the young officer to Philadelphia; Thornton came.

Nor, in this instance, did Bond behave like an alarmist. America was, in the spring of 1794, teetering on the verge of war. Only the quick action of the pro-British party in the United States saved the day for neutrality. The followers of Alexander Hamilton persuaded the President and the senate to open immediate negotiations with England for a commercial treaty. In May, Bond learned to his relief that John Jay as envoy extraordinary was on his way to London.

Meanwhile, Bond had resumed the work of a secret agent. He discovered that France was in urgent need of foodstuffs and that French agents were buying up grain and flour in the United States. For sixteen months, Bond devoted himself to the checking, as he called it, of "a ferocious Enemy." It was frustrating work. Bond collected detailed information on the strength, formation, and destination of French convoys.[46] Although many of his dispatches reached the admiralty before the convoys left the United States, the French managed to elude the Channel Fleet and to reach France safely.[47] As a result, it became Bond's conviction that convoys must be intercepted at the point of departure rather than at their destination. In March 1794, he wrote to Grenville that he could no longer restrain himself from expressing "my sincere Wish that a Squadron of his Majesty's Ships may shortly appear in these Seas."[48]

In the summer of 1794, after three French convoys had sailed, Rear-Admiral George Murray with a squadron of British warships arrived at Halifax.[49] Murray assumed command of the station and henceforth kept several warships at Bermuda and several cruising along the American coast. As the French lost control of United States waters, they abandoned the convoy system. Almost at once, Bond was on to their new tactics. On July 15, 1794, he wrote Grenville that from this time forward the enemy would employ neutral, American vessels, sailing singly, to transport the necessary supplies to France. "The real Destination of the Vessels," read Bond's dispatch, "will be masked under perjured Clearances, and fictitious Papers—for Falmouth—for Poole—for Cowes— and for Bilboa & other Ports of Spain."[50]

That was precisely what the French did. But in spite of Bond's many reports concerning the "neutralized" cargoes, it was the end of April 1795 before the British government took action. Then the King in Council secretly ordered British commanders to seize all provision ships which they might have reason to believe were bound for France. Nonetheless, the French strategem proved remarkably successful. Of one hundred and thirteen shiploads of American provisions, sent by a single French agent, ninety-six arrived safely.[51]

As shipment after shipment got through, Bond returned to a theory he had presented to the Lords of Trade and which he was convinced was "better calculated than any other Measure" to starve the enemy into submission (see Chap. VII). "It suggests itself to me," he wrote to the foreign secretary, "that a heavy Purchase of Grain and Flour to be made here, secretly, under the Authority of his Majesty's Government, might be attended with very beneficial Consequences, and that to whatever Extent the Speculation might be carried, the Advantage to result from it, would far outweigh any Loss which might arise." He urged that the plan be put into immediate effect, confined to a few Persons, perhaps "to one Person here." Although he did not say so, clearly he meant "confined to Mr. Bond."[52]

No answer came. But suddenly, all the frustrations and disappointments connected with Bond's personal battle of the Atlantic no longer seemed important. In May 1795, a letter arrived from

Under-Secretary of State Burges. It was somewhat cryptic; obviously Burges assumed Bond knew more than he did and that certain instructions from Downing Street had already reached Philadelphia. But Bond could read between the lines: Grenville and Jay had concluded a treaty of amity, commerce, and navigation (see Chap. X). For years Bond had believed such an agreement ought to be effected. Now, it existed.

The letter contained even more exciting news. Under-Secretary Aust was about to retire . . . George Hammond was to replace him at the foreign department . . . and Phineas Bond was to become His Majesty's chargé d'affaires in the United States![53] The door to the diplomatic corps had opened. Bond felt no longer confined by limitations. He might climb; he might climb high. He might even become an ambassador.

NOTES

[1]Bond to Grenville, Moore Hall, October 10, 1793, *AHAAR*, 1897, 539.

[2]See Address of the Citizens of Philadelphia to Edmund Genêt, May 17, 1793, *Pennsylvania Gazette*, May 22, 1793.

[3]*Pa. Gazette*, April 24, 1793.

[4]See John Bach McMaster, *A History of the People of the United States from the Revolution to the Civil War* (New York, 1890), II, 100–101.

[5]*Pa. Gazette*, May 22, 1793; for subsequent celebrations see *American Daily Advertiser* (Philadelphia), May 29, 1793; June 3, 1793.

[6]Bond to Grenville, Philadelphia, June 8, 1793, *AHAAR*, 1897, 529.

[7]See, for example, an open letter to the Magistrates of Philadelphia, *Aurora or General Advertizer* (Philadelphia, May 30, 1793).

[8]See *Aurora*, May 23, 1793; June 4, 1793.

[9]See Bond to Grenville, Philadelphia, June 8, 1793, *AHAAR*, 1897, 529, for a description of his work with the British seamen. For his notice see *Pa. Gazette*, May 31, 1793; *Am. Daily Advertiser*, June 1, 1793; *Aurora*, June 1, 1793.

[10]*Pa. Gazette*, June 5, 1793.

[11]See William S. Flory, *Prisoners of War, A Study in the Development of International Law* (Washington, D.C., 1942), pp. 110–132.

[12]Bond to Grenville, Philadelphia, July 7, 1793, FO 5/2.

[13]See enclosures in Bond to Grenville, July 7, 1793, FO 5/2.

[14]*Le Moniteur Universel, Reimpression de l'ancien Moniteur* (Paris, 1840–1844), XXIX, 432–433.

[15]Bond to Grenville, Philadelphia, June 8, 1793, *AHAAR*, 1897, 528–529.

[16]Bond to Grenville, Philadelphia, July 26, 1794, FO 5/6.

[17]See William Laird Clowes, *The Royal Navy, A History from the Earliest Times to the Present* (Boston and London, 1899), IV, 197.

[18]For a general account of the battle see Alexander DeConde, *Entangling Alliance: Politics and Diplomacy under George Washington* (Durham, N.C., 1958), pp. 269–271; for a more detailed description containing figures on tonnage,

types of cannon, and number of broadsides fired see Clowes, *The Royal Navy,* IV, 478; for an eyewitness account by two American seamen on the *Boston* see the sworn testimony of James C. Whitney and Simon Bradbury enclosed in Bond to Grenville, Philadelphia, August 4, 1793, FO 5/2.

[19]See the deposition of Benedict Wheatley, pilot, St. Mary's County, Maryland, May 18, 1793, *ASP,FR,* I, 161; also *Pa. Gazette,* May 15, 1793.

[20]The owners were Robert Findley, Jr., Andrew and George Bacheran, James and Thomas Hopkirk, John Dunlap, and John Bonatyre, *American Daily Advertiser,* June 17, 1793.

[21]Bond to Grenville, Philadelphia, June 8, 1793, *AHAAR,* 1897, 530–531.

[22]See the excellent exposition on American territorial jurisdiction in Charles Marion Thomas, *American Neutrality in 1793, a Study in Cabinet Government* (New York, 1931), pp. 91–117.

[23]See C. S. Hyneman, *The First American Neutrality: A Study of the American Understanding of Neutral Obligations during the Years, 1792–1815* (Urbana, Ill., 1934), p. 89; Bond to Grenville, Philadelphia, July 7, 1793, FO 5/2.

[24]Bond applied the lesson well in negotiating over the *Africa* affair; see the author's "Some Interesting Transactions in Rhode Island," *Rhode Island History* (Providence, October 1960), 97–118.

[25]*International Adjudications, Ancient and Modern, History and Documents,* John Bassett Moore, ed. (New York, 1931), IV, 518–528.

[26]Christ's Church Records, HSP; *Pennsylvania Journal and Weekly Advertiser* (Philadelphia, May 22, 1793). For Bond's role in the affair and for the happiness of the union see Leslie Reade, "George III to the United States Sendeth Greeting . . ." *History Today VIII* (London, November 1958), 775, 780.

[27]Alexander DeConde in his admirable work, *Entangling Alliance,* p. 232 and Charles Thomas in his study of *American Neutrality in 1793,* p. 160 have assumed Hammond handled the case of the *Jane.*

[28]See Knox to Hammond, War Department, July 31, 1793, enclosure C, Bond to Grenville, Philadelphia, August 5, 1793, FO 5/2.

[29]Bond to Knox, Chestnut Street, August 1, 1793, enclosure D, Bond to Grenville, August 5, 1793, FO 5/2.

[30]Knox to Bond, War Department, August 1, 1793, enclosure E, Bond to Grenville, August 5, 1793, FO 5/2.

[31]Hamilton to Grenville, Norfolk, August 9, 1793, FO 5/2.

[32]Bond to Grenville, Philadelphia, August 24, 1793; September 14, 1793, FO 5/2.

[33]Bond to Grenville, Philadelphia, September 14, 1793, *AHAAR,* 1897, 538.

[34]For an excellent account of the epidemic see J. H. Powell, *Bring out Your Dead, the Great Plague of Yellow Fever in Philadelphia in 1793* (Philadelphia, 1949); also see *Pa. Gazette* during August, especially August 28, 1793.

[35]*Letters of Benjamin Rush,* L. H. Butterfield, ed. (Princeton, N.J., 1951), II, 718–719.

[36]Rush to Julia, Philadelphia, September 8, 1793, *Letters of Rush,* II, 655.

[37]Since the death of his grandfather, Bond had been trying unsuccessfully to sell Moore Hall. Tenant farmers cared for two small farms on the estate; but the Hall and two hundred acres remained vacant. See, for instance, the advertisement in the *Pa. Gazette,* February 2, 1791.

[38]Bond to Grenville, Moore Hall, November 8, 1793, *AHAAR,* 1897, 540.

[39]Bond bought the house in his mother's name and through William Lane, realtor, for the sum of £2,350. See indenture, June 1, 1793, CAD COLL, Thomas Cadwalader Section, "Rebecca Bond" Box, and insurance policy, September 11, 1793, Mutual Assurance Company of Philadelphia, on microfilm at

the Custom House, Philadelphia, Pa.

⁴⁰Bond to Grenville, Philadelphia, March 10, 1794, *AHAAR*, 1897, 544.

⁴¹This is the famous order-in-council of November 6, 1793 in which Great Britain again put into effect "the rule of '56": that trade which is illegal in time of peace is illegal in time of war.

⁴²Bond to Grenville, Philadelphia, April 17, 1794, *AHAAR*, 1897, 546.

⁴³Hamilton to Grenville, Norfolk, August 20, 1793; August 25, 1793, FO 5/2.

⁴⁴See *Pa. Gazette,* February 26, 1794.

⁴⁵For the situation in Norfolk and Baltimore see Bond to Grenville, Philadelphia, April 17, 1794, *AHAAR*, 1897, 546.

⁴⁶See Bond to Grenville, Philadelphia, February 20, 1794; February 28, 1794, March 8, 1794, March 23, 1794, April 29, 1794, June 13, 1794, June 20, 1794, June 26, 1794, June 27, 1794, July 1, 1794, July 10, 1794, FO 5/6.

⁴⁷Two of Bond's reports, for example, concerning the first and largest of the convoys reached the admiralty on April 8, 1794. The convoy sailed from the Chesapeake on April 19, 1794. On the 2nd of May, Lord Howe and the Channel Fleet sailed from Spithead to intercept the convoy. A few days later two French fleets put out, one from Brest and the other from Rochefort, to bring in the merchantmen. They engaged Lord Howe who defeated them in the battle of the Glorious First of June; but, on the 14th of June, the great convoy reached Brest without the loss of a single vessel.

⁴⁸Bond to Grenville, Philadelphia, March 10, 1794, *AHAAR*, 1897, 545. Sir John Jervis, then commander in the West Indies, supported Bond's position. He was "grieved," as he put it, over the arrival of the great convoy from Virginia and said that "Had they given me the force I was promised when I left England, not one of those ships would have got out of the Chesapeake. . . ." Quoted by Oliver Warner, *The Glorious First of June* (London, 1961), p. 72.

⁴⁹See Gerald S. Graham, *Empire of the North Atlantic, The Maritime Struggle for North America* (Toronto, 1950), pp. 221–222.

⁵⁰Bond to Grenville, Philadelphia, July 15, 1794, FO 5/6.

⁵¹See Howard C. Rice, "James Swan: Agent of the French Republic 1794–1796," *The New England Quarterly* X (Brunswick, Me., September 1937), 475.

⁵²Bond to Grenville, Philadelphia, June 10, 1795, FO 115/4.

⁵³Bond to Burges, Philadelphia, May 27, 1795, FO 115/4.

CHAPTER TEN

The Consul and the Treaty of Amity, Commerce, and Navigation

John Jay spent the afternoon of Wednesday, the 19th of November 1794, writing letters in his rooms at the Royal Hotel in Pall Mall, London. To Alexander Hamilton he wrote, "My task is done." To Edmund Randolph, "since the building is finished, it cannot be very important to describe the scaffolding." To Rufus King, "I send by the packet the fruit of my negotiation—a treaty." To President Washington, "the treaty . . . is now concluded, and was this day signed."[1]

Jay and Lord Grenville had just affixed their signatures to the first Anglo-American treaty of amity, commerce, and navigation. For five months they had negotiated. Now, as Jay said, the task was done; his mission a success.

But rather than announce the victory Jay would have preferred to rest that afternoon. The dampness in the London air had aggravated his rheumatism; he found it difficult to write. Yet he knew that Grenville, anxious for the treaty to reach America while congress was still in session, had already held the packet boat for over a week and that the ship must go. And so, in spite of continuous pain, Jay wrote half a dozen letters, including a lengthy report for Secretary of State Randolph. By evening the announcements and a signed copy of the treaty were at the post office on their way, Jay assumed, to Falmouth, the November packet, and Philadelphia.

The foreign office too, on that Wednesday afternoon, was occupied with the American mail. For the benefit of Bond and Hammond, Grenville drafted three instructions. He explained that he was himself well satisfied with the treaty and regarded it as the beginning of a new era in Anglo-American relations. In the place of discord and disagreement, he now looked forward, as he worded it, "to permanent harmony and good understanding between the Two Countries in future." And he made it clear that henceforth he expected Mr. Bond and Mr. Hammond "to contribute to the Maintenance of this Good Understanding." The instructions and a copy of the treaty left Downing Street on Thursday, the 20th of November, for Falmouth and the packet boat.[2]

Grenville then turned his attention to other ways of strengthening Anglo-American friendship. It was his conviction that as long as Randolph remained American secretary of state relations between the two countries would continue to be strained. Randolph had publicly and, from Grenville's point of view, "indecently" accused British agents of fomenting the Indian wars along the frontier; he had aggravated the furor over British seizures of American shipping by publishing a false and exaggerated list of vessels taken; and his correspondence with Mr. Hammond constantly breathed "a spirit of Hostility."[3]

The Secretary raised these points with Jay only to learn the American felt as strongly about certain British representatives in the United States. According to Jay, George Hammond's darts had pierced official skins and he wished "Mr. Hammond had a better place and a person well adapted to the existing state of things be sent to succeed him."

The envoy went further. Consuls too, he pointed out, have it in their power "to check or promote conciliation." While saying nothing about Phineas Bond, which under the circumstances was all to Bond's credit, Jay claimed Mr. Hamilton, the British consul at Norfolk, was very unpopular and his character was "far from estimable."[4]

Grenville tended to dismiss the criticism of Hamilton. Bond, who was his superior, thought well of him, and according to the treaty just signed the President of the United States might revoke the exequatur of any British consul at any time and for any reason —even if he took a dislike to the man's face.[5] Since such a procedure was impossible in the case of a minister, whose own country must issue the recall, Grenville regarded the remarks about Hammond more seriously and considered terminating the mission.

Although approving of Hammond's work, the Secretary recognized how difficult the situation had been. The minister "was necessarily . . . much engaged in hostile and irritating discussion." To recall him would indicate a willingness on the part of the British government to cooperate. At the same time a fresh personality, untainted by the recent, unpleasant negotiations, could perhaps operate more effectively and better serve British interests.[6]

There was no problem about Hammond's future; Grenville would promote him to under-secretary of state. The problem was his replacement. Professional diplomats viewed Philadelphia as the worst of all possible assignments. Living expenses there were more exorbitant than in any European capital. Yet the United States was too young a nation to justify a higher rank and salary than that of minister plenipotentiary. Finding the proper person would take time. During the interval Grenville must either keep Hammond on the job or make a temporary appointment. Anxious to demonstrate Britain's sincerity about conciliation, Grenville favored action. Bond was in Philadelphia. The more the Secretary thought about the question, the more convinced he became that even during this delicate period in Anglo-American relations Bond could as charge d'affaires fill the vacancy until the right man was found.

On December 10, 1794, Grenville wrote to Hammond directing him to return to England, to deliver the ciphers and other papers to Mr. Bond, and "to communicate to that Gentleman every information which may be necessary in order to enable him to conduct His Majesty's Affairs in America."[7]

The letter, Bond's commission as chargé d'affaires, and a copy of the treaty left the foreign department in time for the December packet. By that vessel Jay also sent a second, signed copy of the treaty. A third copy he entrusted to David Blaney, an acquaintance, who was on the verge of leaving London for Virginia. That was a fortunate move, for the November mail was still in England. The post office had carefully failed to inform the foreign department that, because of inclement weather, the November packet had never sailed.[8]

She was the *Tankerville,* an old and leaky vessel, so unseaworthy that eight years before her captain had been afraid to take her on a summer crossing. At that time, Temple had sent word to

Whitehall that, if the *Tankerville* got safely home, "she ought never to come out upon another Voyage."[9] Since then she had made countless trips from Falmouth, to Halifax, to New York, and back. Now, on December 14, 1794, carrying both the November and December mails, she weighed anchor for the last time. In mid-ocean a French privateer overtook and burned her. But just before capture the *Tankerville*'s captain, in order to save the mail from enemy hands, threw the diplomatic pouches overboard. The letters Jay had written in pain and haste, Grenville's instructions, four copies of the treaty, Hammond's recall, and Bond's commission sank to the bottom of the Atlantic.

When April arrived without any word of the treaty having reached America, Grenville grew uneasy. It seemed unlikely that both the November and December packets should have miscarried. He was inclined to hold Bond and Hammond responsible for the lack of information.[10] But, early in May, came news of the *Tankerville*'s loss. The post office could no longer suppress the truth, and Grenville became thoroughly apprised. He was angry and disappointed.[11] But both emotions were short-lived. For almost simultaneously came news of the loss of another vessel. She was the *Jean Bart,* a French corvette, carrying the French minister's mail from Philadelphia to Paris. And this time the mail as well as the ship was seized. On Grenville's desk lay Joseph Fauchet's dispatches, and the one marked "number ten" implied that Edmund Randolph was in the pay of the French. If shown to the proper Americans, that letter ought to end Randolph's public career. At once Grenville sent Fauchet's letter, together with duplicate, triplicate, and quadruplicate transcripts of the November and December mails to Philadelphia.[12]

Thus, in the spring of 1795, Bond was officially uninformed about events that had taken place in London six and seven months before. He knew that a commercial treaty between his country and the United States had been signed (see Chap. IX). He also knew from articles in the newspapers that the treaty had reached Philadelphia. But he remained ignorant of its contents.

David Blaney had delivered the unsigned copy early in March. Immediately, the President ordered the senate to reconvene in special session to consider the agreement. But since neither he nor the Secretary of State were as pleased with the provisions as were the negotiators, they kept the document under lock and key in the state department's strong box and not a word about the stipulations passed their lips.[13]

And so Bond waited impatiently for the opening of the special session in hopes he would then become informed. On the 11th of June the senators convened and immediately—to Bond's disappointment—agreed to continue the presidential policy of secrecy. The doors of the chamber closed, and the consul remained in the dark. But within hours of the end of the session on the 26th of June, Bond was in conference with several gentlemen whom he identified as "certain very candid & intelligent Characters here." Being a man of honor, Bond refrained from further description. It became clear from the scope of his report to Grenville that these "intelligent Characters" were United States senators, members of the Federalist or, as Bond always called it, of the moderate party, and that in conversation with the British consul general they had been extremely candid. Less than twenty-four hours after the senate adjourned, Bond was able to write a private letter to Lord Grenville that described in detail the course and results of the special, secret session of the United States senate. Since the debates of that meeting were never published, this particular dispatch—hitherto overlooked by scholars—remains for political historians one of the most important Bond ever wrote.

With a single exception, reported Bond, the general scope of the treaty struck the moderate senators as founded in "Candor & Liberality." The exception was Article XII. The first and second paragraphs permitted United States vessels of seventy tons or less to trade with "His Majesty's islands and ports in the West Indies." For this trade—it may be remembered—Americans had been clamoring ever since the close of the War for Independence. While Bond's informants took no objection to those provisions, their senatorial colleagues in the extremist party regarded the concession as an insult that opened the West Indian trade to mere "canoes" and "fishing smacks." The moderates, on the other hand, were inclined to view the stipulation as an entering wedge that might widen with the passing of time. What gave them pause, wrote Bond, was the third paragraph. For, in order to keep the United States from reexporting tropical goods, it prohibited American vessels from carrying "any molasses, sugar, coffee, cocoa, or cotton . . . either from His Majesty's islands or"—and here was the rub —"from the United States to any part of the world except the United States."

In 1791, or in 1792, or even in 1793, these words might never have raised such "an insuperable Bar;" the southern states were then exporting a negligible amount of cotton. But it was now June 1795: two years after Eli Whitney had invented the cotton gin and when the southern states were turning more and more to cotton production. In 1793, they had exported less than 140,000 pounds of cotton; but in 1794, they sent to Europe a half million pounds; and in the current year they were going to export one and a half million pounds.[14] "A general Restriction [on cotton]," the moderate senators told Bond, "would be too great a Sacrifice, when compared with the Advantage to be gained." They went further. "If Cotton . . . is to be generally restrained," they insisted, "the Commerce of the United States would be put into a worst Situation by the Treaty than it has ever been since the Peace."

Without instructions from England, Bond defended the article as best he could. "It was probably," he replied to the Senators, "never in Contemplation to restrain the Exports of this or any other raw material from the United States, in American Bottoms." For such a provision would be in contradiction to "the Principle of our Navigation Laws [which] encourages the Importation into Great Britain, of the Produce of Any Country, in the Vessels of that Country." But he failed to convince them. The senators answered that even were Bond right and the article modified, there would remain the "insuperable" difficulty of discriminating between cotton from the islands and cotton from the mainland.

In turn, they failed to convince Bond that these were their sole reasons for opposing the twelfth article. "The discussion of this Treaty," read Bond's letter to Grenville, "was carried on with great Warmth on the Part of those, whose Aim it has constantly been to foment Jealousies between the Two Countries—The 12th Article naturally underwent great Investigation." As a result, wrote Bond, "the Moderate Party in the Senate conceived the Addition of the 12th Article of the Treaty would excite much Animosity in the Country and give to the factious Combine which prevail here, Grounds to Censure the Conduct of the Govt." For that reason they moved that the President ratify the treaty, "provided it shall be agreed to suspend so much of the 12th Article as in its Operation, respects the trade to be carried on with His Majesty's islands in the West Indies." In other words, as Bond saw it, the moderates deleted the twelfth article in order to save the treaty.

"The Senate," continued Bond's report, "was full, every Member from every State Attended when the Question on this Resolution was taken:—It was carried by a Majority of 20 to 10." By the bare two-thirds majority required by the constitution.[15]

Bond was pleased. He was as opposed to the twelfth article as were the Americans. For if implemented, it would nullify a phase of his consular work. Bond always supported the Sheffield policy of keeping American shipping out of the Maritime Provinces and out of the British West Indies (see Chap. VII). From the time he commenced his consular duties until 1793, he had been able through facts and figures to prove the efficacy of the policy. Annual statistics showed a decline in United States tonnage and a rise in the number of British vessels engaged in the American trade. But since the outbreak of war with France, the balance had shifted. American tonnage, Bond estimated, had increased by "considerably more than one half." The unfortunate situation was the result of the "embarassed" condition of belligerent shipping. Once peace was restored Britain would regain her supremacy in navigation, provided, Bond kept warning the foreign office, the navigation acts remained in force, and the West Indies remained shut to American vessels.

He had even taken into account that the war might force his government to open the Indies to American shipping. The Caribbean had become an active theater of operations; thousands of His Majesty's troops were stationed in the islands, requiring a steady supply of provisions. If some indulgences to the American trade proved unavoidable, then Bond favored the establishment of one or two free ports as far to the windward as possible and for a fixed period of time. But, he advised Grenville, never permit the Americans direct intercourse with the Indies even in vessels of limited size. For in Bond's own words:

> . . . any limitation of Tonnage, which is to stand as an Article of permanent Compact between the Two Countries, will not avail as a Means of restraining the American Traders in the participation of this beneficial Commerce: If the Size of the Vessels be limited, the Numbers (from the facility of equipping Vessels in the Eastern States particularly) will *soon* be increased in Proportion to the Restriction *on* the Tonnage. This Commerce was almost confined to Vessels, owned in the American Provinces, before the War; and . . . it will return to the American Traders, as soon as the existing Impediments are done away.[16]

And so Bond was delighted the senators were so foolish as to vote down the twelfth article.

But he was all the more anxious to procure a copy of the treaty. The reading of the one article had whetted his curiosity. Since the foreign department had disregarded his suggestions with respect to the West Indies, Bond wondered whether they had ignored his other suggestions and lines of inquiry. Had nine years of work counted for nought? Once again doubts assailed him. This time they were quickly laid to rest. Senator Stephen T. Mason of Virginia deliberately broke the injunction against revealing the treaty's stipulations and gave a copy of the agreement to Benjamin Franklin Bache. On June 29th, an abstract appeared in the Philadelphia *Aurora*. Three days later the entire text was available in pamphlet form. Within the privacy of his own office Bond made a leisurely and thorough study of the document. As he read, he grew increasingly excited. Article after article agreed with his own thinking.

Article VI dealt with the problem that had given rise to his appointment in the first place—the debts owed the British merchants. It provided for a joint Anglo-American commission to examine cases in which British creditors, because of legal impediments, had not as yet received full payment on debts contracted before 1783. The United States government agreed to accept the board's decisions as final and to compensate the British claimants to the total amount of the commission's awards.

Article IX discussed alien land titles, a question that had worried Bond ever since the Harrison case (see Chap. VII). For more than five years he had been urging the foreign office to discourage Britons from speculating in American land companies because, as he put it, "except in the State of Pennsylvania no law exists to enable Aliens to purchase and hold lands" in the United States.[17] Now, the treaty secured those titles. In the ninth article both countries proclaimed that the subjects of either, holding lands in the other, "shall continue to hold them . . . and may grant, sell or devise the same to whom they please, in like manner as if they were natives; and that neither they nor their heirs . . . shall as far as may respect the said lands and the legal remedies incident thereto, be regarded as aliens."

Article XVI justified Bond's warnings about the perennial attempts in the house of representatives to erect a navigation system directed against Great Britain. By that stipulation, the two countries repudiated the placement of discriminatory duties upon the goods, merchandise, and shipping of the other. Article XXIV promised to end the privateer problem that had claimed so much of Bond's time and energy since the outbreak of war with France (see Chap. IX). "It shall not be lawful," read that section of the treaty, "for any foreign privateers . . . to arm their ships in the ports of either of the said parties, nor to sell what they have taken . . . nor shall they be allowed to purchase more provisions than shall be necessary for their going to the nearest port of that . . . State from whom they obtained their commissions."

Nevertheless, Bond found no reference to two subjects he considered particularly important. Nothing in the treaty touched upon British migration to the United States. Yet only recently Bond had written to Grenville reminding him that the American rage for manufacturing continued and that Americans were using every imaginable device "to decoy" artisans from England.[18] Second, the treaty failed to provide for the apprehension and delivery of deserters from His Majesty's ships of war. Bond felt so strongly about that omission, he wrote to Grenville and, "with great Deference," called his attention to it.[19]

Tending to forget that the foreign department had many sources of information other than his dispatches, Bond was inclined to view the treaty as his. It represented, as he saw it, the fruits of his labor, the apogee of his consulship. For personal as well as public reasons he wanted it implemented. But would America accept it?

Although the senate had given its consent, Bond had learned too much about democracy to assume ratification would automatically follow. The President must still sign. And in "this wretched Country," as Bond often described America, "whatever is done by Government must . . . be materially regulated by the probable Effect of the measures upon the Minds of the People." And the people, Bond knew, objected to the treaty.[19]

No sooner was the document published than popular opposition began to crystallize. From the American point of view the treaty gave Britain everything and the United States nothing. "Give up All for Nothing at All" was the way one southern newspaper put it. There was to be no trade with the West Indies; no compensation for slaves and property carried off during the war; no provisions against British seizures of American vessels; no provisions against impressment of American seamen. Yet the United States government was to pay the debts owed the British merchants. In exchange all Britain offered was evacuation of the northwest posts by June 1, 1796. That was like buying a horse twice; twelve years ago Britain had promised to hand over the posts "with all convenient Speed."

Then news broke which seriously imperiled the treaty. A few days after the agreement appeared in print, word arrived that the British were stopping American vessels in the Channel and taking them to English ports. Anti-British sentiment soared. To Americans the seizures meant the British never intended to establish friendlier relations and never had any idea of ratifying a commercial agreement with the United States. Otherwise, asked Americans, why would they elect this moment to insult the stars and stripes?

Bond was mortified. Without instructions from the foreign department he could only guess; but he guessed—again exaggerating his importance—that he was himself largely responsible for the seizures. He had been sending reports to Grenville about French purchases of grain in the United States and the use of neutral American ships to transport the foodstuffs to France (see Chap.

IX). He had been urging government to stop the traffic. He accurately surmised that finally the privy council had taken action and secretly ordered the commanders of His Britannic Majesty's ships-of-the-line to seize all neutral provisions vessels that might be bound for France.[21] As he saw it, in his attempts "to check a ferocious Enemy," he had helped precipitate a crisis that might carry off the treaty for which he had worked long and hard.

Throughout the United States petitions circulated advising the President not to ratify. Up and down the Atlantic seaboard mass meetings protested the agreement. On Independence Day, in the Northern Liberties section of Philadelphia, a mob burned Jay in effigy. The meetings, the petitions, and the British seizures stayed the hand of Washington. "I have never," he wrote to Randolph, "since I have been in the administration of government seen a crisis which, in my judgment, has been so pregnant with interesting events, nor one from which more is to be apprehended. . . ."[22] And in the middle of July, the President left Philadelphia for Mt. Vernon without having signed the treaty.

Preoccupied with events on the national level, Bond found it difficult to concentrate upon routine matters. Nonetheless, consular problems would not wait for the President to decide whether to ratify. In July, Bond was obliged, for instance, to handle the case of Richard Haines. Compared with the fate of the treaty the affair appeared petty; Bond underestimated its significance.

Haines claimed he came from the South Pacific where he had met Thomas Pitt, Baron Camelford, who had given him letters, a Chinese gong, and several valuable paintings to deliver to his family in England. Haines also claimed he had only thirty-eight dollars and needed money and a passage.

The story struck Bond as a complete fabrication. He disliked Haines from the moment he laid eyes on him. The man was "remarkably well made," according to Bond's description, very strong and agile with a mean face that was "lightly pitted" from the small pox . . . and he wore two gold earrings. He looked more like a pirate or an escaped criminal from Botany Bay than the friend of a baron. But error in this case might prove costly; Lord Camelford was Lord Grenville's brother-in-law.

Although Bond suspected Haines of lying, theft, and forgery, he lent him money and procured a passage for him on the *Camilla*. The vessel dropped down river at the end of the month, and Bond thought himself rid of the "obnoxious Character." But not at all. On the 2nd of August, Haines was back, demanding a better ship and more comfortable accommodations. A storm was raging outside; the tides were higher than normal; the rains so heavy they had already washed out bridges and dams and disrupted communications. Bond exploded. Of course, *"Things"* were unpleasant on the *Camilla*. What did Haines expect from any vessel in such "wet and stormy Weather?" Had he waited, conditions would certainly have righted themselves. Instead he had left the ship. Now, the consul general must go to the trouble of booking another passage on another vessel. Bond made it plain that he found this very inconvenient.[23]

Haines finally sailed on the schooner *Nancy*. But nothing could erase the fact that Bond had lost his temper. He had broken a principle sacrosanct to the professional diplomat. It was the three-word canon: Always Remain Calm.[24] Bond would regret the lapse. But in fairness to him the incident had occurred during a critical week in Anglo-American relations.

On the morning of Saturday, the 25th of July, the diplomatic pouch arrived containing the duplicate, triplicate, and quadruplicate copies of the November and December mails. Bond's appointment as chargé d'affaires was official. His spirits rose. Now it was only a matter of days before he would become an active member of the diplomatic corps. That morning Hammond confessed he was pleased his tour was ending—he had never been completely at ease in democratic America—and he hoped that he and his family might be off within a fortnight or three weeks at the most.[25]

More than ever before, both the minister and the consul general wished for a speedy ratification of the treaty; Hammond, because he wanted to take the signed copy with him; Bond, because he was convinced he stood upon the threshhold of a new life. What a triumph for him personally if the treaty were sanctioned just as he was leaving the consular service.

That afternoon, fifteen hundred Philadelphians, by a conservative count, gathered in the State House yard. An old friend of the

Bonds, Dr. William Shippen, chaired the meeting. Twice he read a memorial condemning the treaty. Each time the crowd cheered and waved their hats. When a copy was thrown into their midst and they were told "to kick it to hell," they placed the treaty on a pole and marched around the town. In front of the French embassy, they went through a kind of ceremony apologizing for the "obnoxious agreement." Before the British embassy they burned a copy. From there they trooped up Chestnut Street to Bond's house. Outside the British consulate they shouted denunciations, threw stones at the windows, hurled verbal obscenities at the owner, and burned another copy of the treaty.[26]

Accustomed as Bond was to demonstrations, this "Outrage" upset him. His elation of the morning disintegrated. Now, he wondered whether the treaty would ever be ratified, let alone in the near future. Still there remained one, last move to which Bond and Hammond pinned their hopes: Fauchet's dispatch number ten.

After supper on Sunday, the 26th of July, Hammond read Fauchet's letter to Oliver Wolcott, the American secretary of the treasury. On the next day, having had a certified copy drawn up which he gave to Bond, Hammond handed the original to Wolcott. At once the Secretary of the Treasury handed the letter to Timothy Pickering, the secretary of war. On the night of the 28th, Pickering sat up late translating the dispatch with the help of a French dictionary and a grammar. The next day, Pickering and Wolcott called upon the Attorney General. The three agreed that the President must see the letter. On the 31st of July, Pickering wrote a personal note to Washington asking him "for a *special reason*" to return immediately to the capital and in the meantime "to decide on no important political measure, in whatever form it may be presented to you."[27]

While Bond and Hammond waited for results, the minister prepared for his departure and the consul wrote letters. Bond wrote to Grenville thanking him for the "confidential Trust" his Lordship had placed in him and expressing his "unfeigned Gratitude" for this "very flattering Renewal of his Majesty's most gracious Goodness towards me." He also wrote to every important person he knew in England, informing each of his desire to become minister plenipotentiary to the United States and asking each to use his influence on his behalf.[28]

Washington returned to Philadelphia on the 11th of August and that evening he saw Fauchet's letter. Three days later he handed a signed copy of the treaty to George Hammond. On the 18th, the President received His Britannic Majesty's new representative to the United States. On the 19th, Washington handed Fauchet's letter to Randolph. Randolph resigned on the 21st; and Timothy Pickering became acting secretary of state.

It seemed as though the worst was over, as though Bond was assuming his new duties at a time when the road to "harmony and good Understanding between the Two Countries" was finally clear of obstacles. In the middle of August, Bond was filled with optimism. He expected that the President's ratification of the treaty would "suppress that spirit of Faction and Turbulence which of late has been excited . . . for mere Party Purposes."[29] And he saw himself bringing about the first Anglo-American rapprochement. But as it happened, the next months turned into a kind of nightmare.

In spite of the ratification, opposition to the treaty continued. Jeffersonians claimed Washington had arrogated powers in his handling of the negotiations. The hatred they had directed at Jay turned upon the chief executive himself. Extremists hurled names at the President. They called him "aristocrat" and "tyrant," "the Caesar of America," and the "step-father of his country." There was even talk of impeachment. By September, it was common knowledge the Democrats would carry the fight into the house of representatives. When the fourth congress opened in December, they would control the lower chamber. Plans were afoot to challenge the treaty-making powers as defined in the constitution; to move that, since the Anglo-American agreement was commercial in nature, the President ought to have sought the advice and consent of the representatives; and—what was even more serious—to negate the treaty by voting down the appropriations necessary for its implementation.

Then, too, Randolph remained in the public eye. Instead of slipping quietly into oblivion, he issued periodic statements that he would soon publish a defense which would vindicate his actions and would review "the important Acts of Government for a space of no less than eighteen Months." As a result he became a favorite topic of conversation. Bond overheard many remarks to the effect that Randolph had been unjustly accused . . . that Fauchet had never written the letter . . . that dispatch number ten was forged by the British . . . and that Randolph's defense would undoubtedly reveal "gross Violations of Public and Private Confidence" on the part of Washington's administration.[30]

Disturbing as the gossip was, Bond was even more concerned about the possible contents of the vindication. In certain respects he and Hammond had acted no differently than the French. The British, too, had their sources of information among influential Americans and their intrigues. The question of how much Randolph might know and reveal about British activities in Philadelphia during the past eighteen months very nearly unnerved Phineas Bond.

When he learned Randolph was seeking information about Grenville's instructions to Hammond regarding Fauchet's dispatch and about the length of time Hammond had been in possession of the letter before he delivered it to Wolcott, Bond could no longer remain silent. He waited upon the American secretary of the treasury. In a confidential conversation, Bond told Wolcott that, if Randolph should cast a reflection upon the manner in which His Majesty's ministers had handled the intercepted dispatch, then "I should feel myself in a very delicate Predicament, but, at all Events, called upon in the most pointed Manner to refute such Reflection, unless this Government should come forward and do all that Justice and Candor required."

To Bond's relief Wolcott answered in a "very manly" fashion. The Secretary promised that in the event of any such suggestion he would himself "stand in the Gap and disclose to the World, every Fact, of which this Government was in possession."[31]

Bond could go no further; he must simply wait for publication. But summer gave way to autumn without the appearance of the vindication. The suspense proved almost unbearable. The possible ramifications frightened Bond. If Randolph attacked the British with force, Bond could foresee enough votes joining the extremist side in the house to kill the treaty.

Then, too, it seemed as though his own countrymen were playing into the hands of the Jeffersonians. During August 1795, one unpleasant diplomatic incident followed another: at the beginning of the month, the British warship *Africa,* allegedly two miles off the Rhode Island coast, stopped and searched the American coastal vessel *Peggy* in an attempt to seize the private papers of Joseph Fauchet . . . Bond's uncle, Thomas William Moore, the British vice-consul at Newport, became involved in a controversy with Governor Arthur Fenner and as a result lost his exequatur . . . at the end of August, the *Africa,* flying French colors and again supposedly within American waters, impressed three seamen off a United States ship.

In handling these incidents Bond impressed upon the Americans how much he lamented "that any accident should have happened, to interrupt that Harmony, and good Understanding, which was just beginning to dawn between the Two Countries."[32] He was successful in preventing the affairs from growing out of proportion and rupturing Anglo-American relations. Nonetheless, the negotiations dragged into December, giving rise to a voluminous correspondence and to innumerable conferences between Bond and Secretary of State Pickering.

While in a state of anxiety over the treaty, Bond was forced to work as never before. Not only was he in almost daily communication with Pickering and Wolcott, but as chargé d'affaires he was obliged to maintain a more vigilant watch over American political developments and to report more frequently and in greater detail than when he had been merely consul. Bond had never been niggardly about writing dispatches—during his ten-year consulship he had sent an average of twenty-one letters a year to the foreign department. But now, during his ten-month tenure as chargé d'affaires, Bond wrote fifty-nine reports and several were pamphlets in size.

Also, there were social obligations. As the representative of His Britannic Majesty, Bond was expected to entertain American statesmen and politicians, members of other foreign legations, as well as important visitors who came to town. Although the functions consumed further time and energy, this was one aspect of his work Bond enjoyed. It pleased him to have the English drawing room on the second floor of the Chestnut Street house filled with guests, and while they sipped tea or coffee around a fire blazing behind the shining grate, to regale them with anecdotes about public and private characters. Unfortunately, not everyone found Bond amusing. One young traveler upon returning to England described in detail his discomfort and "shame," in his own words, "at seeing the representative of my country playing the part of a political mountebank before many of the principal persons of the American metropolis."[33]

Last, there were consular duties. The foreign department failed to provide for a successor in the consular office. For months Bond was obliged to function both as chargé d'affaires and consul general. "I did hope," read a private note he wrote to Under-Secretary of State Aust, "I should have been permitted to have appointed some Person Consul here at a small salary, who could have gone thro' all the formalities of the office, and have reported to me, as principle in any particular exigency." The pathetic plea eventually produced results. But communications in the late eighteenth century were slow. The year was ending before Edward Thornton arrived and relieved Bond of the consular work.

By then other pressures had lifted. At long last, on the 18th of December, Randolph's vindication came off the press. Although the former Secretary implied British machinations had brought about his downfall, his defense as a whole was a weak and sniveling performance. Instead of assuming the offensive, Randolph threw himself upon the reader's sympathy and whined over his misfortune. Instead of directing his fire at the British, he sniped at the President.[35]

Within three days Bond was able to report that the publication "has operated very perceptibly, here, in diminishing the Inveteracy, which heretofore, marked the Conduct of the Party, to which the late American Secretary of State was attached: Every man of that Party," continued Bond, "seems willing to let this ruined Bark sink of itself, and to shun the Vortex, which hurries it to the Bottom."[36]

Bond could breathe again. The fate of the treaty no longer

worried him. Although the great debate over the granting of appropriations remained to be heard, Bond was now convinced the house would confirm the agreement. He argued that as long as Randolph had failed to arouse passions, reason would prevail. Withholding of appropriations by the house could lead to the dissolution of the constitution of the United States, and "for that end," wrote Bond, "the Leaders of the democratic Party, with all that Spirit of Division & Discontent, which marks their Conduct, are not yet ripe."[37]

But as the outlook for public affairs brightened, Bond's personal prospects dimmed. On the 8th of February 1796, the diplomatic pouch arrived containing, among other documents, the following announcement:

Downing Street, Novem: 4th 1795

Sir/

The King having been pleased to destine [sic] Mr. Liston, at present his Majesty's Ambassador at the Porte, to succeed Mr. Hammond,

I have to destine [sic] that you will communicate this circumstance to the members of the American Government, and will at the same time express His Majesty's confidence that this appointment will not fail to be agreeable to that Government.

Mr. Liston is presumed to be now on his return from Constantinople, and will shortly after his arrival in this Country prepare to embark for America by the earliest conveyance.

I am
        Sir
            Your most obedient
                humble Servant
                    Grenville[38]

The letter was disheartening. For the distance from chargé d'affaires to minister plenipotentiary was far shorter than from the office of consul general, and Bond had hoped that if he put forth extraordinary effort he would be appointed minister to the United States. Now, after months of unremitting labor he must again sink into the ranks of the consular service; he must, as he saw it, wait for the next ministerial interim and for the chance of becoming chargé d'affaires a second time.

However disappointing the announcement was, even more discouraging news followed. Through friends in England Bond learned Richard Haines' story had proved true; the letters he carried were genuine; and Haines, as Bond could well imagine, had complained bitterly to my Lord Grenville about the treatment he had received from the British consul general at Philadelphia.[39] Then, on the 25th of March 1796, fell the harshest blow of all.

Until that black Friday, faith in the excellence of his performance as chargé d'affaires had sustained Bond. He reasoned that an unblemished record would triumph over the recent setbacks and ultimately carry him into the diplomatic corps. But on Friday, March 25, Bond discovered he had failed as chargé d'affaires to do that which he ought to have done; he had committed a sin of omission.[40]

The error had occurred in September 1795, when Bond was functioning in a dual capacity. He was worried about Randolph's vindication and about the treaty. He was negotiating over the affair *Africa*. He had just discovered that American merchants on the pretext of requiring protection from Caribbean pirates were arming their vessels, sailing them to the West Indies, and there selling them to the French as privateers. The United States government was demanding explanations about continued British seizures of American shipping. And Bond was involved in clearing a cartel ship of French prisoners of war. At that moment, the American press announced the conclusion of a treaty at Greenville with twelve Indian tribes of the Northwest Territory. In a lengthy report about other matters, Bond mentioned the Indian agreement and had his clerk enclose a copy of the articles.[41] But pressed for time and assuming perhaps that a pact with savage tribes could hardly affect the affairs of civilized nations, Bond failed to study the document.

Six months later he wished he had. To his acute embarrassment the British secretary of state must point out to Phineas Bond that the treaty of Greenville contradicted the Anglo-American treaty of amity, commerce, and navigation. In a nine-page letter Grenville explained that the eighth article of the Indian treaty, prohibiting any person from trading with the Northwest Indians unless furnished with a license from the United States government, was inconsistent with the third article of the Anglo-American treaty which stated "it shall at all times be free to His Majesty's Subjects and to the Citizens of the United States, and also to the Indians dwelling on either side of the Boundary line, freely to *pass and repass* by land or inland *Navigation* into the *respective Territories and Countries of the two parties on the Continent of America . . . and freely to carry on trade and Commerce with each other*." The contradiction was particularly serious, continued Grenville, because the Indian agreement was concluded "so long after the period when the British Treaty had arrived in America," and because "the period is now approaching in which His Majesty has stipulated that His forces should evacuate the Posts on the American side of the Boundary line."

Detailed instructions followed. Bond was to deliver to the American government an enclosed memorial. It described the contradiction and requested the addition of an explanatory article to the Anglo-American treaty, "by which it shall be declared," read Grenville's memorial, "that no treaty subsequently concluded by either party with any State or Nation whether European or Indian, can be understood in any manner to derogate from the rights of free intercourse and commerce secured by the . . . treaty of Amity, Commerce and Navigation." Grenville further instructed Bond that no other form than an additional article would be acceptable to "His Majesty's Confidential Ministers," and until the conclusion of such an article there would be no evacuation of the northwest posts.

Attached was a credential empowering Bond to negotiate the explanatory article, but, at the same time, Grenville ordered him to ignore the commission. "As I have reason to believe," read the dispatch, "that Mr. Liston . . . will be able to proceed shortly to America and as it is probable that a Negociation [sic] of this Nature may be conducted with greater Prospects of success by a Minister . . . you will defer acting upon the instruction . . . as long as a delay may be practicable. . . ."[42]

Grenville no longer trusted Bond. The Indian treaty had cost him the confidence of the foreign department. Sensing—what, indeed, proved true—that he would never be able to regain the lost position, Bond wished now to leave the consular service, and as soon as possible. Feverishly he searched for an avenue of escape. The one he hit upon was the St. Croix river commission.

The peace treaty of 1783 had defined the St. Croix river as the northeastern boundary between British North America and the United States. Shortly afterward, when it was discovered that different maps labeled different rivers flowing into the Passamaquoddy Bay as the St. Croix, a dispute developed. The disagreement involved thousands of square miles of land. In order to resolve the problem Jay and Grenville provided in their treaty for a joint commission to determine the boundary line.[43] It was this international board of adjudication that offered Bond a way out.

Eight days after he received Grenville's instructions, Bond sent a private letter to his Lordship requesting the appointment as His Majesty's representative on the boundary commission. He knew acceptance meant loss of his tenure in the consular service; he knew too that as commissioner he would be obliged to explore a region that remained for the most part rugged wilderness. Bond, who always dressed impeccably and if possible avoided a trip by stagecoach or passenger vessel, was so desperate he convinced himself that travel in a birchbark canoe clothed in buckskins would prove "an enjoyable relaxation."[44]

During the next weeks he threw himself into the new role. He collected maps and diaries by early French and English explorers. He spent hours reading Samuel de Champlain's descriptions of his voyages around the Bay of Fundy and his discovery of the island and river which he named the St. Croix. Bond pored over ancient land grants and board of trade reports. After a period of intensive research, he reached the conclusion that the river which the natives called the Schoodiac was in reality the St. Croix, and he drew up a scholarly brief supporting the thesis.[45]

Meanwhile, he was obliged to pursue his official duties. The great debate over the Anglo-American treaty was underway in the house of representatives. It had become a constitutional crisis. For the basic issue, as President Washington put it, was not whether the British treaty was a good or a bad treaty, but whether there ought to be any treaty without the concurrence of the house.[46] Bond followed the debate and described it for the benefit of the foreign department. He also delivered Grenville's memorial about the Indian treaty. In April, at Pickering's insistence, he entered into half-hearted negotiations over the explanatory article. Grenville's letters had quashed his initiative. Determined to live by the letter of his Lordship's instructions, Bond tried to drag out the negotiations so that Liston might conclude them.

But on the 30th of April, by a majority of one vote the house of representatives confirmed the Anglo-American treaty. Pickering then became very anxious to conclude the article. Delay, he argued, would be dangerous. Tennessee was about to enter the union. The explanatory article must be submitted to the senate before two more Jeffersonian Democrats joined the upper house. Since there was still no word of Liston's arrival, Bond reluctantly acquiesced.

Aside from a few disagreements over the turning of a phrase, the negotiations moved smoothly. By the 2nd of May, the article was written and Pickering was urging Bond to sign. He insisted on waiting for Liston. On the 4th of May, Pickering again asked Bond to sign; again Bond refused. He had just heard that Liston had arrived in New York. Somewhat annoyed, Pickering agreed to wait for twenty-four hours. On the 5th, Bond received a letter from Liston. He was planning to leave New York on the 6th or 9th of May. That, claimed Pickering, would be too late, and, therefore, on the 5th of May 1796 Phineas Bond signed his name to the explanatory article.[47] On the 9th, the United States Senate by a vote of nineteen to five advised the President to ratify.

Immediately Bond notified the Canadian officials that they might proceed with the transfer of the posts. He also wrote to Liston explaining why he was obliged to complete the negotiations. The new minister took no offense. Seven years older than Bond, he was accustomed to titles and honors. "I . . . cannot help approving," read Liston's answer, "in consideration of the circumstances of the moment, your determination to conclude & subscribe the article respecting the American Treaty with the Indians, without waiting for my arrival."[48]

Thus Bond helped to bring about the first Anglo-American rapprochement. The signing of the explanatory article, clearing the way, as it did, for the transfer of the northwest posts, established "Harmony and Good Understanding" between the United States and Great Britain. During the next years relations between the two countries continued to improve while Franco-American relations deteriorated. Yet Bond found small satisfaction in the achievement; once again his hopes were shattered. No sooner had he handed over his seals and ciphers to Robert Liston than Thomas Barclay arrived in Philadelphia. He was a former American Loyalist, currently a resident of Nova Scotia, and he had just received his commission as British representative on the St. Croix river board. Bond hid his disappointment. He even went out of his way to help Barclay. The consul handed over the documents he had collected and the brief he had written. They proved helpful to the commission and were partially responsible for the ultimate decision that the Schoodiac was the true St. Croix river.

But it was a disillusioned Bond who returned to the office of consul general. For the next three years he put in a perfunctory performance. His dispatches were without suggestions and new ideas. They confined themselves to routine, consular matters such as the granting of Mediterranean passes, the exchange of prisoners of war, and the assistance given to distressed British seamen. Bond transferred his energies from public to private affairs. He concentrated upon his law practice which he began to share with his nephew, Thomas Cadwalader. And he again proved his prowess as a matchmaker. David Montague Erskine, the son of Bond's friend and kinsman, visited Philadelphia. Bond took a liking to young David Montague, entertained him and introduced him to the family. To Bond's delight, his niece, Fanny Cadwalader, and David Montague Erskine fell in love and were married at Christ's Church on the 16th of December 1798.

Bond's relations with Robert Liston and his wife, Henrietta, were friendly. And the Bonds and the Listons enjoyed a close, social connection. Mrs. Liston became very fond of Bond's mother and of his sister, Williamina. Bond saw to it that the Listons were comfortable. He supplied them with good Madeira and porter. He advanced to Liston, whose salary was often in arrears, large sums of money.

Liston, in turn, did what he could for Bond. When Sir John Temple died of apoplexy in November of 1798, Liston wrote to Grenville urging a return to the former organization of the consular service and the appointment of Bond as consul general for all the United States. But Grenville preferred keeping the service, as he put it, "on its current footing,"[50] and he appointed Thomas Barclay as Temple's successor at a salary of £1,500 a year. When Bond learned this, both he and Liston wrote protesting that the salary of the consul general for the eastern states was larger than that of the consul general for the middle Atlantic and southern states. Within a few months, Bond received a notice from Grenville that "His Majesty has been most graciously pleased to direct that your Salary should be made equal to that of His Majesty's Consul General for the Eastern States, and should take place from the Date of that Gentleman's Appointment to that Office."[51]

Friendly as Bond and the Listons were, when the minister received his recall, it was not Phineas Bond but Edward Thornton who was appointed chargé d'affaires. Bond knew then that he had had his chance and it would never recur. He became reconciled to his fate. He confessed to Liston that for several years he had been aware of "ill-founded gossip" about himself. Although he despaired of tracing it to its source, he admitted that it "has been successful as to its Motive: else how can I account for the Dissolution of that Influence which I flattered myself I had established, by a Course of the most unremitted Attention to my Duty . . . To me the Effect has been Serious," continued Bond, "but not so serious as it must be to those who look for Advancement:—I am content with the Station in which I am placed, & when any untoward Accident shall separate me from my Family, I can accommodate myself to an humble & aeconomical Retreat, in that blessed Land to which I owe all the Good I ever have or ever shall possess."[52]

NOTES

[1]John Jay, *The Correspondence and Public Papers of John Jay*, Henry P. Johnston, ed. (New York, 1893), IV, 134–137.

[2]Grenville to Hammond, Downing Street, November 20, 1794, *Instructions to British Ministers*, pp. 68–75.

[3]Grenville to Hammond, Downing Street, November 20, 1794, *Instructions to British Ministers*, pp. 73–74.

[4]Jay to Grenville, Pall Mall, London, November 22, 1794, *Jay's Corr.*, IV, 147.

[5]Article XVI of the treaty provided for the exchange of consuls and stated ". . . that, in case of illegal or improper conduct towards the laws or Government, a Consul may either be punished according to law, if the laws will reach the case, or be dismissed, or even sent back, the offended Government assigning to the other their reasons for the same." In jest, Grenville said this meant that the president might dismiss a consul if he took a dislike to the man's face. See John Quincy Adams to Timothy Pickering, London, December 5, 1795, *Memoirs of John Quincy Adams Comprising Portions of his Diary from 1795 to 1848*, Charles Francis Adams, ed. (Philadelphia, 1874), I, 157.

[6]Bradford Perkins, *The First Rapprochement, England and the United States 1795–1805* (Philadelphia, 1955), pp. 44 and 197.

[7]See *Instructions to British Ministers*, p. 77. For the difficulty of filling the American post and the foreign department's decision to keep Bond as chargé until a minister could be found, see the notation dated, July 8, 1795, Gouverneur Morris, *The Diary and Letters of Gouverneur Morris*, Anne Cary Morris, ed. (New York, 1888), II, 101.

[8]See *Treaties and Other International Acts of the United States of America*, Hunter Miller, ed. (Washington, D.C., 1931), II, 267.

[9]See Temple to Carmarthen, New York, June 7, 1786 and September 7, 1786, FO 4/4.

[10]Grenville to Hammond, Downing Street, April 15, 1795, *Instructions to British Ministers*, p. 80.

[11]See, for instance, Grenville to Jay, Dover Street, May 11, 1795, *Jay's Corr.*, IV, 174.

[12]Grenville to Hammond, Downing Street, May 9, 1795, *Instructions to British Ministers*, p. 83; Perkins, *First Rapprochement*, p. 36.

[13]Although several copies of the treaty circulated clandestinely in Philadelphia, there is no evidence that either Bond or Hammond was able to procure one. See Edmund Randolph, *A Vindication of Edmund Randolph, Written by Himself and Published in 1795* (Richmond, 1855), p. 18.

[14]Holland Thompson, *The Age of Invention, A Chronicle of Mechanical Conquest* (New Haven, 1921), p. 49.

[15]Bond to Grenville, Private, Philadelphia, June 27, 1795, FO 115/4. When the senate rose they lifted the injunction on the secrecy of the session but, at the same time, the senators enjoined themselves not to disclose the contents of the treaty.

[16]Bond to Grenville, Philadelphia, November 23, 1794, *AHAAR*, 1897, 560–563.

[17]Bond to Leeds, January 3, 1791, *AHAAR*, 1897, 472; Bond to Grenville, July 7, 1793, FO 5/2; November 23, 1794, *AHAAR*, 1897, 566.

[18]Bond to Grenville, Philadelphia, August 16, 1795, FO 115/4.

[19]Bond to Grenville, Philadelphia, August 16, 1795, FO 115/4.

[20]Bond to Grenville, Philadelphia, June 27, 1795, FO 115/4. For a lively account of the popular opposition to the treaty see John Bach McMaster, *A History of the People of the United States* (New York, 1892), II, 246–250; 254.

[21]Secret order-in-council, April 25, 1795.

[22]Washington to Randolph, Private, Mount Vernon, July 29, 1795, *The Writings of George Washington*, Jared Sparks, ed. (Boston, 1836), XI, 48.

[23]For the Haines affair see Bond to Grenville, Philadelphia, July 29, 1795, and August 8, 1795, FO 115/4.

[24]See Harold Nicolson, *Diplomacy* (London, 1958), p. 116.

[25]Leslie Reade, "George III . . . Sendeth Greeting . . .," *History Today VIII* (November 1958), 780; Randolph to Washington, Philadelphia, July 29, 1795, Sparks, *Wash. Corr.*, XI, 42.

[26]See Pickering to Washington, Philadelphia, July 27, 1795, Charles W. Upham, *The Life of Timothy Pickering* (Boston, 1873); III, 183; Wolcott to Washington, Philadelphia, July 26, 1795 and to Mrs. Wolcott, Philadelphia, July 26, 1795, George Gibbs, *Memoirs of the Administrations of Washington and John Adams, Edited from the Papers of Oliver Wolcott, Secretary of the Treasury* (New York, 1846), I, 217–218.

[27]See Gibbs, *Wolcott*, I, 232; Upham, *Pickering*, III, 187–189.

[28]Bond to Grenville, Philadelphia, June 30, 1795; Bond to Under-Secretary of State Aust, Private, Confidential, Philadelphia, July 29, 1795, FO 115/4; Sir George Jackson to Bond, Upper Grosvener Street, London, August 27, 1796, CAD COLL, PB, "West New Jersey" Box.

[29]Bond to Grenville, Philadelphia, August 16, 1795, FO 115/4.

[30]Bond to Grenville, Philadelphia, August 24, 1795, September 29, 1795, October 11, 1795, November 5, 1795, November 15, 1795, FO 115/4.

[31]Bond to Grenville, Philadelphia, September 29, 1795, FO 115/4.

[32]Bond to Grenville, Philadelphia, September 13, 1795, FO 115/4.

[33]Thomas Twining, *Travels in America One Hundred Years Ago, Being Notes and Reminiscences* (New York and London, 1900), pp. 39–40.

[34]Philadelphia, July 29, 1795, FO 115/4.

[35]William Cobbett prefaced his review of the *Vindication* with the following verse:

> For gold defiles by frequent touch;
> There's nothing fouls the hand so much.
> But as he paws he *strove to scower,*
> He washed away the chemic power;
> And *Midas* now neglected stands,
> With *ass's ears* and *dirty hands.*

Selections from Cobbett's Political Works, John M. Cobbett and James P. Cobbett, eds. (London, n.d.), I, 85.

[36]Bond to Grenville, Philadelphia, December 20, 1795, FO 115/4.

[37]Bond to Grenville, Philadelphia, March 31, 1796, FO 115/5.

[38]FO 115/4.

[39]Bond to Hammond, Private, Philadelphia, September 24, 1796, FO 115/5.

[40]See Grenville to Bond, Downing Street, January 18, 1796, *Instructions to British Ministers,* pp. 106–110.

[41]Bond to Grenville, Philadelphia, September 29, 1795, FO 115/4.

[42]Grenville to Bond, Separate, Downing Street, January 1796, *Instructions to British Ministers,* p. 110; the order was repeated onApril 3, 1796, FO 115/5.

[43]Article V.

[44]Bond to Grenville, Private, Philadelphia, April 2, 1796, FO 115/5.

[45]See Bond to Grenville, Philadelphia, May 3, 1796, FO 115/5.

⁴⁶Washington to Edward Carrington, Philadelphia, May 1, 1795, Sparks, *Wash. Corr.,* XI, 122. For the best secondary account of the debate see Perkins, *First Rapprochement,* pp. 39–42. Bond reported in detail on March 28, 1796, March 31, 1796, April 7, 1796, April 17, 1796, FO 115/5.

⁴⁷See Bond to Grenville, Philadelphia, May 6, 1796, FO 115/5; Miller, *Treaties,* 347.

⁴⁸Liston to Bond, New York, May 9, 1796, Liston Manuscripts, National Library of Scotland, Edinburgh, ACC. 720, Box XII also on microfilm, Library of Congress, Washington, D.C.

⁴⁹Barclay and Bond maintained a spirited correspondence through the summer of 1796. See *Selections from the Correspondence of Thomas Barclay formerly British Consul-General at New York,* George L. Rives, ed. (New York, 1894), pp. 48, 52, 54, 60–66.

⁵⁰Hammond to Liston, Downing Street, January 26, 1799, Liston Mss., Box XIII.

⁵¹Bond to Grenville, Philadelphia, November 27, 1798, FO 5/25; November 3, 1799, FO 5/26; Grenville to Bond, Downing Street, February 1799, FO 5/26.

⁵²Bond to Liston, Philadelphia, January 2, 1802, Liston Mss., Box XIV.

CHAPTER ELEVEN

The Consul
and British Policies

At the beginning of the nineteenth century, the capital of the United States moved from the banks of the Delaware to the banks of the Potomac, but Phineas Bond remained in Philadelphia. Ten years earlier the capital had come to him. Now it had gone, leaving Bond in the backwater. He was no longer the consul at the hub of national activities, no longer the man on the spot to whom the British government might turn during an emergency or ministerial interim. Knowing, as he did, that Grenville had cooled toward him, Bond thought his days of influence were over. He reconciled himself to an unexciting future. He resolved that henceforth instead of being married to his post, he would, like other consuls, look upon it as a mere job. He even contemplated semiretirement and toyed with the idea of living outside the city at "Solitude," John Penn's bachelor retreat on the west side of the Schuylkill river.[1]

But in the spring of 1801, Bond received official notification that Pitt's administration had, after seventeen years, come to an end.[2] In February, Henry Addington had become first minister and Robert Banks Jenkinson, Lord Hawkesbury, later the second earl of Liverpool, had replaced Grenville at the foreign office. Hawkesbury was the son of the former chairman of the Committee for Trade for whom Bond had done a great deal of work. The father, Bond knew, thought well of him; perhaps the same would prove true of the son. At least there was a chance now that the foreign department would pay more attention to the dispatches from Philadelphia. Bond felt the resurgence of hope and with it the return of that old resilience which was so characteristic of him. Thoughts of retirement vanished. Once again Bond was married to His Britannic Majesty's consular service, as devoted as ever to "Work, King, and Country."

As soon as he learned about the changes at the foreign department, Bond began collecting statistics on the number of British emigrants arriving at American ports. He was as convinced as he had been sixteen years ago when the Edemson and Royle case (see Chap. VI) broke that unless the migration of British capital and citizens to the United States ceased, America would become a great manufacturing nation. He had never stopped warning the foreign office of the potential danger. But he had over the years despaired of finding an effective way of checking the flow of British capital to America. Still he clung to his conviction that parliament by placing restrictions on passenger vessels could curtail British emigration to the United States. He had laid his legislative plan before Carmarthen and before Grenville. The former had done nothing; the latter had gone so far as to instigate an order-in-council preventing "Artificers, Manufacturers . . . His Majesty's Subjects from embarking on Board Foreign Ships or Vessels for the purpose of quitting this Kingdom and going into Parts beyond the Seas. . . ."3 To Bond that was but a halfway measure.

And so he again raised the issue. In July 1801, Bond wrote to the new Secretary of State that "there have, already, arrived this Summer in the Delaware from Belfast, Newry, and Londonderry, about 1200 Passengers." In August, he reported that 7,575 passengers had arrived in Philadelphia during the current year from Ireland, England, and Wales.

Bond appealed to Hawkesbury's reason by emphasizing the connection between British migration and American manufacturing; he also played upon the Secretary's emotions and sympathies. The letters from Philadelphia described the "putrid & filthy Conditions" on the passenger vessels, the lack of food and water, and the startling number of mortalities. Out of one hundred and two passengers on the *Adventure* from Liverpool, reported Bond, fifty-three died on the crossing and nineteen were ill when the ship reached the Delaware. "These deluded Emigrants," read his dispatch, "seduced by Assurances that they would reach . . . their

Destination in six weeks, laid in Provisions, accordingly:—the Vessel had upward of nine Weeks passage—those who perished may literally be said to have been starved." But, pointed out Bond, if the vessels were obliged to meet certain standards, the casualties could be avoided, and as the passenger traffic became less profitable, the number of emigrants would decline. For the third time, the consul submitted his program for a parliamentary bill to regulate the passenger trade.[4] This time he met success.

His Grace the Duke of Argyle, president of the Highland Society, was as concerned as Bond about emigration. Economic distress in Scotland was driving large numbers overseas. Although at first the exodus appeared healthy, a beneficial way of draining surplus population, by the late nineties whole areas were deserted. The Highland Society then began to press for an end to emigration. Carrying, as they did, considerably more weight with government than the consul in Philadelphia, the house of commons responded to their pleas and appointed a committee in 1802 to survey the situation. In the following year the committee reported that Highland emigration "is fast approaching to the Point of complete Depopulation of a large District of the Kingdom" and recommended it be discouraged by regulating the vessels carrying passengers from the United Kingdom to foreign ports.[5]

On June 24, 1803, parliament passed Britain's first Passenger Act.[6] Since the law contained every important regulation proposed by Bond, those who drew up the bill probably had access to his dispatches. He had asked that the number of passengers on each vessel be limited in proportion to the ship's burthen. The act limited the number to one adult, or one child, or one member of the crew for every two tons of burthen. It further stipulated that when a vessel carried cargo, then the number might not exceed one person for every two tons of the *"unladen"* part of the ship.

Or again, Bond had proposed that parliament define the nature, the quantity, and the amounts of provisions to be dispensed daily "for the Consumption of the Passengers." The act ordered that every vessel for North America be stored with at least twelve weeks of food and of "good and wholesome water," in sufficient quantities for a daily allowance of not less than one-half pound of meat, one and one-half pounds of bread, half a pint of molasses, and one gallon of water for "each and every person on board."

Bond also suggested that the law require a surgeon or apothecary of "competent Abilities" to sail on each vessel in order to care for the sick and to supervise the sanitary conditions. "No ship or vessel," read the Passenger Act, "carrying 50 persons or more should be cleared unless she carries a Surgeon," who possesses a certificate that he has passed the examinations at the Surgeon's Hall in London, or at the Royal College of Surgeons at Edinburgh, or at Dublin. He must bring with him a "properly stored" medicine chest; he must keep journals; he must see that all bedding is aired daily during the voyage and that the vessel is fumigated with vinegar at least twice a week.

Infractions of any of the provisions carried heavy fines. The captains were obliged to bond their vessels for seaworthiness, and the vessels were also subject to search and examination by officers of His Britannic Majesty's ships of war. The Passenger Act was, for Bond, a triumph. Within two years, he was able to report that as a result of the law the passenger traffic had almost ceased.[7]

But months before Bond learned of the bill's passage, war with Napoleon had reopened and the consul had fixed his attention upon another old "line of Enquiry": the policy of impressment which he had helped formulate in 1793 (see Chap. VIII). Again his reasoning was rooted in fear of the potential power of the United States. " 'Tho but an Infant now," was Bond's constant cry, eventually America will outrival Great Britain in commerce, in trade, and in manufacturing. To cripple American navigation, it was imperative to press seamen off United States vessels; for the increase in American shipping was frightening.

In 1803, Bond reported that United States tonnage amounted to 917,000 tons; in 1804, it advanced to 983,000 tons; in 1805, "it had increased," wrote Bond, "to the enormous Size of 1,084,900 Tons."[8] He maintained that British seamen had made this "baneful Effect" possible. For Americans, Bond pointed out, were not a maritime people. New Englanders, in his own words, "who retain the Spirit of their Ancestors, breed their Children to the sea . . . but it is not so in the middle & southern States, where a false Pride prevails, and it is thought humiliating to train their Children in this line."[9] As a result Bond claimed that one-third, perhaps one-half, of the crews sailing from ports outside New England were British.

"For very few British Seamen," as he put it, "are now left who were resident in or were employed in the Service of the United States during the War." Those few, in Bond's eyes, were *bona fide* Americans. Not so the rest. The majority remained subjects of His Britannic Majesty regardless of any naturalization rites or oaths of citizenship they might have performed. They were born within the king's dominions. As a result, according both to Bond and to British law, such subjects owed the king natural allegiance, which could not "be forfeited, cancelled, or altered by any change of time, place or circumstance." That part of British law was particularly meaningful to Bond. At great personal sacrifice he had himself lived by it (see Chap. II). It disturbed him that from greed, or cowardice, or both, British seamen would desert "the Country which gave them Birth," and would sail under the stars and stripes, contributing "essentially," as he worded it, "to the Advancement of a foreign Navigation."[10]

Such sailors were deserters. They must be reclaimed. For as always, Bond insisted that although Britain might win the war, she would lose the peace were the United States to gain a monopoly of the world's carrying trade (see Chaps. VII and VIII). Until he wrote his last dispatch, Bond championed Britain's right to press. He never appreciated how the practice trampled upon the national honor and integrity of the United States. Nor did he recognize that with the passing of time an increasing number of Americans were reaching the position "that war was the only alternative to national humuliation and disgrace."[11] Bond kept assuring the foreign department that the United States would never go so far as to declare war. A rupture would hurt Great Britain, he wrote, but it would prove "absolutely ruinous" to America.[12] Although British ministries rose and fell during the first decade of the nineteenth century, there was no relaxation in the policy of impressment. Thus in some small measure Bond helped to confirm one of the policies that led to the War of 1812.

But long before that occurred, there was another and very different kind of problem that claimed his attention. Each summer he found himself writing either, "I am extremely sorry to Inform your Lordship, that the Mayor of Norfolk in Virginia, has announced the Appearance of the Yellow Fever in that Town . . .," or, "Some cases of the Yellow Fever have recently appeared in the City of New York . . .," or, "It is with great Concern that I inform Your Lordship that a putrid contageous Fever prevails in the City of Charles town, in the State of South Carolina . . .," or, what was still worse, under the heading of Germantown or Chestnut Hill, "I removed hither . . . as a Place of Shelter, from the Yellow Fever, which prevails in Philadelphia."[13]

During August, September, and October of each year, Bond devoted himself to the plague. He was determined to do everything possible to prevent its introduction into the British Isles. He personally examined all vessels in the Delaware that were bound for a British port. Although the Philadelphia Board of Health might proclaim the city healthy, if Bond knew of a single case, he would refuse to clear ships. Even when the city was, in his opinion, genuinely free of disease, he examined all freight; for some part of a cargo might have been where fever existed. Such practices offended captains and merchants. Infuriated, they brought pressures to bear upon the consul, but to no avail. Bond stood by his principles. Still he appreciated how difficult it was to withhold attestations and questioned whether other British consuls in America were as strict as he.

Bond raised the point with the foreign department, warning them that clean bills of health were only partially trustworthy. "The only secure Means," wrote Bond, "of guarding against the Introduction of this Disease, will be to subject every Vessel, arriving in the King's Dominions from Ports where malignant Fevers do, or are supposed to exist, to a close Examination, during that Season in which those diseases have commonly prevailed."[14]

Again Bond's warnings, coupled with those from other sources, found their way into the statute books. In the spring of 1805, parliament passed a quarantine measure that required "*All* ships & vessels that have touched at any place where His Majesty and Privy Council should have adjudged it probable that plague or other infectious disease may be brought should go into quarantine."[15] The act further prohibited the unloading of any vessel which, having performed quarantine in a foreign lazaretto, arrived at a British port with clean bills of health. Until the privy council had examined the ship's papers and issued an order "directing the unloading," no person, no goods, and no merchandise might leave the vessel.

With the passage of the quarantine law, Bond could flatter himself that some action had been taken on every major issue he had raised. But he had given all he had. There was nothing left for him to offer and he was too old to hit upon new ideas. Bond was now entering his late fifties and his health was failing. He suffered from what the doctors called "nervous debility." With the passing of time the attacks of the mysterious malady increased in intensity and frequency. By 1807, Bond could no longer keep the truth from the foreign department; he admitted in one of his official dispatches that he was ill.[16]

With the breaking of his health he grew testy. His reports contained an increasing number of attacks on Jefferson, on the Democratic party, and on the United States in general. Bond described Jefferson as the most unscrupulous of politicians, as the devoted admirer of Bonaparte and of everything French. Bond went so far as to claim that the President wished for the extermination of Great Britain and that, in the consul's own words, "There is no revolutionary Degradation England could endure that would not gratify his Feelings."[17]

Bond always opposed the Democrats. He had disliked Jefferson ever since the battle of the memorials over the debts, when Jefferson had defeated Bond at his own game (see Chap. VIII). Yet in the past Bond had maintained perspective. Never before had he stooped to such vitriolic denunciations as those that now filled his letters. They, too, were different. They were either brief to the point of terseness or long and rambling. Often they were inaccurate. Bond was obliged to send corrections on previously submitted figures and statistics. Sometimes he was obliged to confess that a piece of information he had stated as fact proved to be merely an erroneous rumor.

Nevertheless, he stayed in Philadelphia. He must atone for that rash act he had committed over a quarter of a century ago when he had deserted his family to serve his king (see Chap. II). Never again would he leave them without a "male Protector." But in 1809, the situation changed. Bond's family began to break up.

On the 30th of January 1809, Bond's mother died at the age of eighty-two. Her death left Bond and his spinster sister, Rebecca, alone in the house on Chestnut Street. Still, while there were other members of the family nearby, Bond hesitated to leave. In Philadelphia there was Bond's sister, Elizabeth Travis, and her five children; his favorite sister, Williamina; his nephew, Thomas Cadwalader and his wife, Mary. Furthermore, in Washington there was Bond's niece, Frances Cadwalader Erskine.

In 1806, the British government appointed David Montague Erskine envoy extraordinary and minister plenipotentiary to the United States. Since their arrival, the Erskines and the Bonds had maintained close and affectionate relations. The men were fond of one another in spite of their political disagreements. Erskine was a Fox man; Bond, a Pittite. Erskine was a Whig; Bond, a Tory. Erskine wished to conciliate America and establish friendlier relations; Bond objected to any accommodation that might involve the surrender of a British right or principle.

Thus while Erskine was negotiating an agreement in Washington that would lift Britain's orders-in-council and facilitate trade for the Americans, Bond was sending letters to George Canning, who was then secretary of state, urging him not to relax "the Pressure upon the Rights of Neutrals."[18] For various reasons, far more complex than Bond could perceive, the orders remained in force. The British government repudiated Erskine's agreement and recalled the minister in disgrace.

For personal reasons, Bond was sorry. The departure of the Erskines further divided the family. Bond's sister, Williamina Cadwalader, was unwilling to be again separated from her daughter and grandchildren. She decided to follow the Erskines to England and to make her home there.

Bond then set his affairs in order. His mother had left her entire estate to him with the understanding that he would provide each of her surviving daughters with a house and a lot. In the autumn of 1809, Bond gave to Elizabeth Travis, to Williamina Cadwalader, and to Rebecca Bond, ten thousand and one dollars each. They in turn released him from any further claims on their mother's estate.[19]

Bond also prepared to hand over his legal practice. Since he had been sharing it for years with Thomas Cadwalader, his nephew was well prepared to take over and handle the cases. Nonetheless, it was necessary to transfer the powers of attorney. That took time.

Not until the summer of 1810 was Bond ready to request a leave of absence. His last leave, he pointed out in the letter to the foreign department, had been seventeen years ago. He wished to return now because of the precarious state of his health, "which," he wrote, "has rendered me anxious to try the Effect of a Change of Climate, and of some little Respite from Business." Six months later, Bond received "his Majesty's gracious Permission, to return to England."[20]

Rebecca, of course, would accompany him, and Bond decided also to take his niece, Ann Travis, who was then eighteen years old. He arranged for the rental of the house on Chestnut Street. He made his last will and testament, leaving all his personal effects, wines, liquors, jewelry, and books together with the sum of five thousand pounds sterling to Rebecca. He left five hundred pounds to Thomas Cadwalader and fifty pounds to his wife, Mary Biddle Cadwalader. The remainder of the estate Bond bequeathed to his two sisters, Williamina Cadwalader and Elizabeth Travis, and to their heirs.[21]

Since Bond always thought in terms of the family, he left the consular office in the hands of his cousin, Thomas William Moore, son of the former vice-consul for Rhode Island. On the 8th of June, Bond formally invested Moore with the office of proconsul. At the end of the month, Bond, and Rebecca, and Nancy, as they called Ann Travis, Bond's personal valet, and several of the women servants sailed for England.

It was the worst passage Bond had ever endured. He was ill the entire time and, although he had paid what Rebecca considered "an enormous price," the accommodations were poor. The cabins were small and crowded and the ship was literally stuffed with cotton. Bales of the white stuff filled every possible space and even hung over the sides. "We had not room," wrote Rebecca, "to take exercise . . . and in the small space that the *greedy owners* allowed us to walk in we had the agreeable noise & effluvia of the hen coops & ducks—happily . . . the weather was fine & we could sit upon Deck on the only seats we had, the hen coops."[22] It was fortunate for Bond that the weather held and the trip was short. For when the ship reached Liverpool at the beginning of August, he was so feeble he was forced to remain there for over a week before journeying by slow stages to London.

There the Bonds lived for a few months in what Rebecca described as "excellent lodgings" on St. Albans Street. Then, at the beginning of 1811, Bond purchased a furnished house. It was No. 19 Baker Street, a large place with a stable, a coach house, and other outside buildings. The main dwelling had three drawing rooms and a mass of beautiful furniture. Even in the servants' quarters there were curtains around the beds.[23]

Bond's health improved slightly. He was able to do some work at the Temple and to enjoy a few of the many calls and invitations. The Penns, the Listons, the Erskines, former Under-Secretary of State Aust called, as, to Bond's great pleasure, did the Duchess Dowager of Leeds. The merchant companies whom Bond had represented entertained him. Lady Ball, widow of the former Governor of Malta, gave a dinner party in honor of Bond. And the great Mrs. Siddons, whom Bond always admired and who also lived on Baker Street, included the Bonds whenever she gave one of her famous garden parties. There were visits in the country to the Erskines at Holmbush, to the John Penns at Stoke, and to the Barclays at Berry Hill.

Then in August 1812 came news that the United States had declared war on Great Britain. Bond's heart broke. He had thought it would never happen. Now that it had, he considered himself responsible for the tragedy. "He looks ten years older," wailed Rebecca, "than he did three days ago." In the following year, Frances Erskine found him "very much altered, indeed." She wrote to her brother, Tom, that Uncle "is older in *every respect* than Grandmamma was just before she died."[24]

Bond's health worsened steadily. He was seldom free of pain. Gout added to his misery. Whenever he tried to work he suffered an immediate setback. By 1814, he knew he had no chance to get well. He left the house only for brief rides and only because they were recommended by his physicians. Then he was obliged to grasp the arms of a servant for support. For the last six months of his life Rebecca never enjoyed a full night of rest. For the last five weeks she never left Bond's chamber.[25]

At nine o'clock on Friday evening, the 29th of December 1815, Phineas Bond died. On the following Saturday, he was buried in the churchyard at Middle Temple. His coat of arms was hung in the great hall. There it remained until the war of 1939 when a bomb destroyed that part of the building.

The passing of Bond coincided with the passing of an age. At Vienna and at Ghent the negotiators had made peace. The Anglo-French wars were over, as was the War of 1812. Henceforth, Great Britain would move closer to France, to the nation whose name Bond had, throughout his life, spelled with a small "f" and whom he had always regarded as "the ferocious Enemy." At the same time, negotiations and compromise would characterize Britain's relations with the United States. Bond had served his era well, but it too had gone.

NOTES

[1]See Bond to Liston, Philadelphia, February 2, 1801 and January 2, 1802, Liston Mss., Box XIV and XV.

[2]Lord Hawkesbury to Bond, Downing Street, February 20, 1801; Bond to Hawkesbury, Philadelphia, June 3, 1801, FO 5/33.

[3]Order-in-Council of April 8, 1795. See Grenville to Hammond, Downing Street, April 15, 1795, *Instructions to the British Minister*, p. 81.

[4]Bond to Hawkesbury, Philadelphia, July 13, 1801, August 11, 1801, FO 5/33.

[5]See the excellent discussion by Helen I. Cowan, *British Emigration to British North America, the First Hundred Years* (Toronto, 1961) pp. 22–23, and *Parliamentary Reports, Sessional Papers, House of Commons*, (London, 1803) IV, 32–33, 38.

[6]43 Geo III c. 56.

[7]See Bond to Lord Harrowby, Philadelphia, March 4, 1805, FO 5/46. The shipping interests considered the Passenger Act too harsh. The requirement to carry a surgeon caused genuine hardships, for there were times when vessels were

unable to sail because they were unable to procure the services of a physician. See Stanley C. Johnson, *A History of Emigration from the United Kingdom to North America 1763–1912* (New York, 1914), p. 104.

[8]Bond to Lord Howick, Philadelphia, February 1, 1807, FO 5/53.

[9]Bond to Hawkesbury, Philadelphia, February 1, 1804, FO 5/43.

[10]See Sir William Blackstone, *Commentaries of the Laws of England in Four Books,* William Draper Lewis, ed. (Philadelphia, 1897), I, 369.

[11]See Norman K. Risjord, "National Honor as the Unifying Force," *The Causes of the War of 1812,* Bradford Perkins, ed. (New York, 1962), p. 95.

[12]See, for instance, Bond to George Canning, Philadelphia, August 2, 1807, FO 5/53.

[13]See Bond to Hawkesbury, Rockwell near German Town, October 4, 1802, FO 5/36; Bond to Hawkesbury, Rockwell near German Town, October 4, 1803, FO 5/39; Bond to Harrowby, Philadelphia, September 26, 1804, FO 5/43; Bond to Hammond, Philadelphia, September 7, 1805, FO 5/46.

[14]Bond to Hawkesbury, Philadelphia, September 13, 1803; Rockwell, October 4, 1803, FO 5/39.

[15]45 Geo III c. 10.

[16]Bond to Lord Howick, Philadelphia, March 28, 1807, FO 5/53.

[17]Bond to Howick, Philadelphia, March 28, 1807, FO 5/53.

[18]See, for instance, Bond to Canning, Philadelphia, May 3, 1808, FO 5/59.

[19]See indentures, October 5, 1810, Record of Deeds, IC 11, 702.

[20]Bond to Lord Wellesley, Philadelphia, September 1, 1810, February 2, 1811, FO 5/71, 5/78.

[21]See invoice of Hume & Etting Co. for auctioning of Bond's household furniture, June 29, 1811, CAD COLL, PB, "Voucher" Box; Bond's will in "Biog." Box.

[22]Rebecca Bond to Mrs. Thomas Cadwalader, Liverpool, 5th, 1811, CAD COLL, Thomas Cadwalader Section, "Rebecca Bond" Box.

[23]See Rebecca Bond to Mrs. Thomas Cadwalader, London, February 1, 1812, "Rebecca Bond" Box.

[24]See Frances Erskine to Thomas Cadwalader, 19 Baker Street, May 27, 1813, "11 T" Box.

[25]Rebecca Bond to Thomas Cadwalader, London, August 16, 1814, January 2, 1816, January 9, 1816, CAD COLL, Thomas Cadwalader Section, "Rebecca Bond" Box.

CHAPTER TWELVE

Bond and the
British Consular Service

Bond had the distinction of being the second British consul to the United States. He arrived at Philadelphia shortly after the American Revolution and remained there on active duty for a quarter of a century. On a day-in-day-out basis he proved to be a first-rate consul and more than any other official was 'responsible for the growth, development, and organization of the British consular service in the United States.

In Bond's time the service was one of the most difficult branches of government in which to work. Although more than three hundred years old, it remained inchoate.[1] It was largely unorganized, unregulated, and unsystematized. There were no fixed policies with respect to salaries, fees, promotions, retirements, nor leaves of absence. What was even more confusing for those who served, the duties of a consul remained undefined (see Chap. VI). No parliamentary acts regulated consular functions. There were no consular manuals nor handbooks. Since the foreign department failed to prepare written instructions, Bond and other British consuls went on their missions without written directives. They had for the most part to learn their jobs on the spot with little help or guidance from the home authorities. At the same time they were obliged to work for many different masters and many different departments of government.

The Consul's Superiors in England

Bond's supreme master—and he would have had it no other

way—was His Britannic Majesty. George III assented to the opening of a consulate at Philadelphia, approved the appointment of Bond, and authorized the foreign department to commission him. Although the king's signature failed to appear on Bond's credentials, the papers were written in the royal name. "George the Third," read Bond's commission, "by Grace of God, King of Great Britain, France & Ireland, Defender of Faith . . . To all and Singular to whom these Presents shall come, Greeting—." An explanation for the opening of the consulate followed; then the words that clarified the relationship between consul and king. "We," the commission continued, "reposing special Trust and Confidence in the discretion and Truthfulness of our Trusty and Welbeloved Phineas Bond Esquire . . . do by these Presents nominate, constitute, and appoint the said Phineas Bond to be our Consul to the States of New York, New Jersey, Pennsylvania, Delaware and Maryland."[3] In other words, Bond held his office from and at the pleasure of His Britannic Majesty. Before leaving on his mission the consul waited upon King George, bade his sovereign farewell, and kissed the royal fingertips (see Chap. IV).

The power of the purse cemented the relationship. During the initial negotiations over the office, the foreign department attempted to save the monarch money. Under-Secretary of State Frazer suggested to Bond that the merchants, of course, would pay his salary. The gambit, which had never in the past worked too successfully, failed in this case. Without a salary from the government Bond was prepared to turn down the appointment. In the face of his opposition the foreign office acquiesced and entered Bond's name on the civil list with a third class rating.[4] For the remainder of his life Phineas Bond was paid from the personal funds of George III and as a result was a member of the royal household.

Another superior was His Britannic Majesty's principal secretary of state for the foreign department. Bond's appointment originated with the secretary of state, then the Marquis of Carmarthen. It was he who interviewed Bond, approved his qualifications, worked out the style and form of the appointment, and signed the commissions. Moreover, in accordance with established procedure, as consul Bond had to address and send all official dispatches to the secretary of state; in turn he received the majority of his instructions from the secretary of state. He was the official, above all others, whom Bond must satisfy.

Although during the first sixteen years of his tour there were only two secretaries of state—Carmarthen and Grenville—during the next nine years, Bond had to work under eight different secretaries.[5] As a result, he then turned more and more to the under-secretary of state.

When Bond joined the consular service, the foreign department consisted of several clerks, a single under-secretary, and a secretary of state. The under-secretary was William Frazer. Before leaving on his mission Bond spent six months at Whitehall working closely with Frazer on the problem of the Mediterranean passes and on the question of organizing the consular service in the United States. Frazer remained a friend and an ally until he retired in 1789.

Then the foreign department gained an additional under-secretary. For the remainder of Bond's tour there were two under-secretaries of state; after 1793 one was responsible for American affairs.[6] He handled far more of the consular correspondence from the United States than the secretary of state, whose attention was called only to those reports of special interest or significance. Occasionally consular instructions went out in the name of the under-secretary. Fortunately, Bond managed to establish amiable relations with these officers.

The first under-secretary for American affairs was James Bland Burges with whom Bond got along well. The second was Bond's close friend, George Hammond.[6] Although the consul continued to address his official dispatches to the secretary of state, he bared his soul to the under-secretaries. With Burges, for instance, Bond broke down and confessed how confused he was over consular functions and how desperate was his need of money. He always approached the under-secretaries for help in obtaining a promotion or a salary raise.

Since in the first decade of the nineteenth century it seemed as though every notice from London announced another change in ministry and the appointment of another foreign secretary, Bond increased his correspondence with the under-secretary. On questions that demanded immediate action Bond sent personal letters to George Hammond. When, for instance, John Wallace, the vice-consul at Savannah, died, Bond at once wrote to Hammond urging a "speedy" replacement in this "Port of considerable Trade" and recommending Wallace's brother for the office. Or again, as critical political situations arose, Bond reported them in detail to the under-secretary.[7]

Still there were other masters whom Bond must serve. While all his dispatches went directly to the foreign department, many were for the benefit of other departments. When those letters arrived, the foreign office clerks immediately made copies for the officials concerned. To the Committee for Trade, for example, went copies of Bond's reports on American harvests, on the prices of American grains and flours, on the duties collected by American customs officers, on the amount of foreign tonnage entering United States ports, and on the size of the American merchant marine. From 1789 until 1791, Bond worked almost exclusively for the Committee for Trade, gathering the information they required for the all-important report on the American situation (see Chap. VII).

In similar fashion Bond served the Lords of the Admiralty. For them he kept a register of all Mediterranean passes issued in his consular district. He also kept a register of all British ships and vessels arriving at the Philadelphia port; he noted the dates of their sea papers, the names of the vessels, the names of their masters, their destinations, and the number and description of their crews. Twice a year he sent those records to England. Also to the admiralty went Bond's reports on shipwrecks and naval engagements off the American coast, as well as receipts for exchanges of prisoners of war. Then too most of Bond's work as a spy was for the benefit of the admiralty lords (see Chap. IX). For them he collected information on the formation of convoys, on the naval strength and maneuvers of the enemy, and on the possible destinations of hostile fleets and ships of war.

Bond had also to work for the privy council. All of his reports on questions that threatened the well being of the British Isles went at once before the council. Thus Bond's dispatches on the yellow fever and on the Hessian fly, the insect that was damaging American wheat crops, were laid before the King in Council. In both cases action immediately followed. In June 1788, for instance, the council prohibited until further notice the importation of American grains. Later, the ministers ordered the quarantining of vessels and cargoes arriving from the United States in an attempt to prevent the introduction of yellow fever into the United Kingdom.[8]

Last, Bond worked for the treasury lords and the customs officers. One of his prime duties was the protection of British revenue. That involved the policing of the British navigation acts. Thus inspection of cargoes, certification of sea papers, manifests, and freight registers became part of Bond's routine functions. For various reasons this was the area of operations in which his actions provoked the most frequent reprimands.

His district was large. Yet in person he was only able to cover the port of Philadelphia. Through no fault of his, many harbors within the area remained unsupervised. To solve the problem Bond arranged for British traders resident at those ports to function as consular agents, to prepare sea papers, testify to the landings of cargoes, and issue Mediterranean passes. Other than the rewards of prestige, there was no remuneration for the work. As might be expected, some of the merchants proved careless; irregularities resulted.[9]

While the treasury lords were fast to condemn noncompliance with parliamentary acts, they were slow to furnish consuls with copies of bills. Lack of information became a universal consular complaint.[10] Even Bond, who out of his own pocket paid Charles Dilly, the London book dealer, to send copies of all bills dealing with commerce, found himself at times ignorant of the law and erring because he was uninformed of the latest regulations.

In 1794, for instance, the customs in Scotland criticized the forms they were receiving from Bond's district dealing with the landing of bonded goods. The certificates, they claimed, were too terse and failed to give the shipping marks and numbers, the precise quantity, and the person by whom shipped and to whom consigned. Or again, four years later, Bond received a reprimand from the treasury lords; tobacco manifests from his command failed to indicate where the hogsheads had been taken on board.[11] In both cases Bond acted quickly. He prepared forms that met the new requirements and at his own expense had them printed and distributed to all consular officers and agents in his territory.[12] Although costly, the procedure silenced the critics.

There were also those outside government whom Bond must please. No British consul might overlook the British merchants. The very existence of the service depended upon trade. In Bond's case there was also a specific group of traders whom he must never neglect—the Committee of London Merchants Engaged in the North American Trade.

They had recommended him to the foreign office; he had obtained his appointment through their influence. While owing the committee as a whole a debt of gratitude, he owed even more to those members who had during his long years of exile given him legal work, the representatives of the twenty-one largest houses trading with the middle Atlantic and southern states. They were the prime movers behind his consulship. Before he was even commissioned, Bond had agreed with those particular merchants that, were he to go to Philadelphia as consul, he would function there as their "confidential Person in a public Capacity" (see Chap. IV). The welfare of his merchant clients always remained uppermost in Bond's mind. Yet relations with them caused him some embarrassment.

No sooner had he assumed his official duties than his merchant friends began to press upon him powers of attorney. But Bond, who in so many ways typified the late eighteenth century bureaucrat, in this instance reacted in a modern fashion. Although many consuls engaged in private enterprises—the majority, having been recruited from the mercantile ranks, traded—Bond argued that because of possible clashes of interest it would be improper for him to practice law while holding a public office (see Chap. V). The opinion placed him ahead of his times. Very few people, if any, considered such activities as lacking in propriety. Bond himself only withstood the pressure from his former clients for thirty months. Then, swamped as he was with financial problems, he succumbed. For the remainder of his tour Bond served the British merchants as a whole in the role of consul at Philadelphia and individual merchants in the role of private attorney.

Bond worked for a multitude of masters, but he enjoyed one important advantage; for the most part his superiors were in England, three thousand miles away. In America, Bond's masters were few in number and they proved to be neither oppressive nor demanding.

The Consul's Superiors in America

When Bond arrived in the United States in 1786, Sir John Temple was already stationed at New York City as consul general for all the United States. Hence before proceeding to Philadelphia, Bond was obliged to wait upon Sir John, present his credentials, and acknowledge Temple as his immediate superior in America. But as it happened, that ceremony represented Bond's first and last act of deference to the consul general.

The two men disliked each other at sight (see Chap. V). After the initial meeting they elected to avoid one another. Since at the time all consular officers, regardless of rank, reported directly to the secretary of state, it was possible for the consul and consul general practically to sever relations. Temple could have kept in close communication with his junior officer. He could, for instance, have demanded special reports and research from Bond and, instead of ignoring him, could have made his life miserable.

Perhaps Sir John ought to have pursued a different policy. In the spring of 1793, Bond was promoted to consul general for the middle and southern states; Temple was demoted to consul general for the New England states. Thereafter, as far as the British consular service in America was concerned, Bond had no superior.

Before the promotion occurred, however, George Hammond, the first British minister to the United States, arrived in Philadelphia. Secretary of State Grenville left no doubt in Bond's mind that the minister plenipotentiary outranked the consul. In a letter announcing Hammond's appointment Grenville wrote to Bond that "I must particularly desire that you will, on every Occasion in your Power, afford him [i.e., Mr. Hammond] that Assistance and show him that Attention which both his personal Merits and the Situation in which he is placed so justly entitle him to."[13]

Bond followed orders. He worked closely with Hammond and with Hammond's successor, Robert Liston. In each case, instead of a master-servant relationship, mutual collaboration characterized the connections between consul and ministers (see Chap. VIII). These amiable relations were largely owing to Bond's efforts. He went out of his way to be generous. He gave Hammond, for instance, the use of his house on Second Street and went even further and found him a wife.

The pattern repeated itself with the Listons. Bond's mother and Henrietta Liston grew very fond of one another. Bond carefully looked after the minister's comforts. Indeed, had it not been for the consul, the Listons might have had a most difficult time. The exigencies of war caused the British treasury to default on the payment of diplomatic salaries. When Liston found himself hardpressed for money, Bond came to the rescue, advancing the minister sums of considerable size.[14]

Liston was the last British minister with whom Bond was closely associated. After the capital of the United States moved to the District of Columbia, Bond was no longer in the same city with the representatives of His Britannic Majesty. With the British diplomats who followed Liston, other than David Montague Erskine, Bond had practically no relations.[15] Because of family ties, the Erskines made frequent trips to Philadelphia and corresponded with Bond. But other ministers found it unnecessary to visit Pennsylvania and equally unnecessary to negotiate with the British consul there.

Finally, in the United States, Bond must serve the admiral in command of His Majesty's North American squadron. The consul must keep the admiral informed about enemy naval maneuvers, about rumors of war and peace, and about important political developments. Late in 1795, for example, a rumor spread that Spain would soon enter the war against Great Britain. Bond then received an order from Admiral Murray that, if the rumor proved true, "you will be good enough to send me as early Accounts of it as possible by way of . . . Norfolk; and likewise hire a vessel to send notice to me or the Commanding Officer at Bermuda."[16]

Bond hired many a pilot boat to carry messages to the commander of His Majesty's ships of war off the American coast only, in most cases, to learn that his efforts had been in vain; the fleet had sailed. Murray and his successors were distant and elusive masters.

Bond had only a few superiors in the United States. At the same time he was himself superior to many and almost a law unto himself.

Bond and the Consular Service in America

When Sir John Temple was commissioned in 1785, the foreign department had no plans for other consuls to follow Sir John. To them Temple's appointment represented a kind of trial balloon. Only after agreeing to commission Bond was the foreign department prepared to develop a program for the consular service in the United States. Since Bond was the man on the spot, they sought his advice.

Because of the vastness of the distances and the slowness of communications, he suggested that the foreign office should abandon the idea of a consul general for all the United States and instead divide the country into consular districts. The officer in charge of each would be responsible for all consular business and personnel within his command. For all practical purposes the districts would operate as autonomous units. France and the United Netherlands had adopted this system for their services in America.[17] Without troubling to change Temple's title, Secretary of State Carmarthen accepted the plan.

The Marquis had Bond commissioned consul for the middle Atlantic area, responsible for New York, New Jersey, Pennsylvania, Delaware, and Maryland. Shortly after Bond left England, the foreign office appointed George Miller consul for the Carolinas and Georgia. During Bond's tour and largely owing to his recommendations, five consular districts came into being—the New England, the middle Atlantic, the district of Virginia, of the Carolinas and Georgia, and of Louisiana.

The number of consuls also increased. While Bond was only the second British consul to America, when he left Philadelphia in

1811 on what proved to be his final leave of absence, there were twelve British consuls in the United States. Of the twelve, eight were part of Bond's command, organized in the following manner:

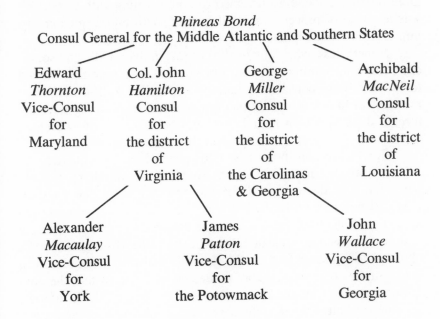

Phineas Bond
Consul General for the Middle Atlantic and Southern States

Edward *Thornton* Vice-Consul for Maryland

Col. John *Hamilton* Consul for the district of Virginia

George *Miller* Consul for the district of the Carolinas & Georgia

Archibald *MacNeil* Consul for the district of Louisiana

Alexander *Macaulay* Vice-Consul for York

James *Patton* Vice-Consul for the Potowmack

John *Wallace* Vice-Consul for Georgia

For the majority of the British consulates in America Bond was indirectly, if not directly, responsible. Six of the officers who served were indebted to him for their credentials. He had literally —under the direction of the foreign department—drawn up and signed their commissions. Two vice-consuls received their quarterly salaries from Bond. For three years he paid Thomas William Moore at Newport, Rhode Island, and Edward Thornton at Baltimore, Maryland, from his own funds and then submitted an account to the secretary of state, entitled, "Extraordinary Disbursements in Sterling money incurred on his Majesty's Service."[18] The treasury was slow to reimburse; Bond finally persuaded the foreign department to relieve him of what had become an onerous duty.

He also, contrary to Temple's practice, was in constant communication with those officers nearest to Philadelphia. He required the consuls in Virginia and Maryland, for instance, to keep him fully informed on economic, political, and military developments at their ports. Although Hamilton, the consul in charge of the Virginia district, became accustomed to collaborating with Bond, this was less true of officers stationed farther south and at greater distances from Philadelphia.

Nonetheless, when any of the consuls in the middle and southern command required a favor, a promotion, or a raise they turned to Bond. Always considering himself responsible for the welfare of the men in his territory, he made a point of intervening with the foreign department on their behalf and, when their safety seemed threatened, took measures to protect them (see Chap. IX).

For the responsibilities he had assumed Bond ultimately received a fair remuneration. But he found his initial salary of £700 per annum inadequate, and for the first five years the consular post cost him money. He had then no expense account and no right to charge consulage, that is, fees for services such as certifying a manifest or issuing a clean bill of health. The British merchants objected to consular fees on the grounds that they amounted to a tax on trade. At times the foreign department agreed that the government rather than the merchants ought to pay consular salaries; at other times it seemed to the department only just that the traders who benefited most from the presence of consuls should contribute to their salaries. As it happened during Bond's tour, the foreign office was implementing the mercantile point of view, providing the consuls in America with what they considered to be generous salaries, and in exchange prohibiting them from charging fees. Bond never during his twenty-five years of active duty collected the usual consular emoluments.[19]

Without consulage and without an expense account, he found £700 a year insufficient. Upon submitting vouchers, the treasury would reimburse him for money spent on distressed British seamen, on collecting information, and on trips taken in the line of duty. But there was no reimbursement for a copy clerk, whose salary came roughly to £100 a year, for entertainments which in the absence of a minister proved expensive; and there was no reimburse-

Emoluments
ment for postage. The cost of stamps bothered all consuls.[20] Though the British packets carried the official mail free of charge, Bond, for instance, must have the pouch carried from Philadelphia to New York. He was obliged to maintain a wide correspondence throughout the United States and to communicate with His Britannic Majesty's ships-of-the-line, with the governors of Canada, of the British West Indies, and of the Maritime Provinces. Bond had also to pay for his stationery. Then, too, he discovered it was impossible to submit vouchers for certain sums he had spent. Success as a consul depended upon his sources of information and the most valuable sources were secret. Their identity must never be revealed.[21]

Thus Bond had been on the job only a short time when he began to plead for an expense account. Finally, in 1792, he won an additional £200 per annum for exceptional contingencies. Other raises followed until his salary reached £1,672 a year. That was about eight thousand dollars, three thousand more than the American foreign secretary received.[22] With such remuneration Bond had no quarrel. He was then able to live graciously, even elegantly.

Privileges and Immunities

The consulship offered still other advantages. The most important for Bond personally was the ability to visit America. The consular commission, written in the name of His Britannic Majesty, enabled him to return. Once the United States government had accepted the credentials and issued an exequatur, he was able to remain without fear of arrest on the old charge of treason.

That marked the extent of the diplomatic immunity he enjoyed. For unlike a minister, Bond as consul was subject to punishment under the laws of Pennsylvania and of the United States in civil as well as in criminal matters. Furthermore, no special protection extended to his mail, nor to his house, nor to his person.[23] When he encountered for the first time the ire of the Philadelphia merchants and manufacturers, Bond was justly afraid the mob might break into the consulate to seize his papers and perhaps to harm his person. He fled to New York City (see Chap. VI).

From that experience he learned to take precautions with the consular pouch. He never again entrusted his official dispatches to the United States post office, but instead arranged with private messengers to carry the pouch to New York and to see it safely on the packet boat.[24]

During his long tour Bond faced many disturbances. He grew accustomed to insults hurled by angry crowds, to raised fists, and to stones smashing the windows of the consulate. He ceased to worry about his personal safety and he never again ran away, largely because he knew that in its own way the city had come to accept him.

In 1807, following the *Chesapeake* and *Leopard* affair, the ugliest of all demonstrations occurred. In Bond's own words, "indecent Tunes were played before my House, late at Night—a few Panes of my Windows were broken, and a noisy crowd, after committing some Outrages upon a British . . . Brigantine, in this Port, unshipped her Rudder, and paraded it twice in the Course of one Evening before my Door, where they attempted to burn it. . . ." But, continued the letter, "I should be wanting in Justice to a vast Number of the most consequential People here, if I were to omit expressing my Sense of the firm, candid, and honorable Part they took in discountenancing any Threat, or Offer of Violence, contemplated towards me."[25] By 1807, in short, "a vast Number" of citizens had come to respect Phineas Bond, the person.

Without time on his side Bond would never have been able to win that esteem. But in his day, time was something upon which British consuls could depend. It was unwritten custom that tenure accompanied an appointment. Consuls generally remained at their original station until the receiving government revoked the exequatur—an infrequent occurrence—or until, like Phineas Bond, they were overcome by sickness or by death.

Functioning in a Dual Capacity

Over the years, what meant the most to Bond was the opportunity the consulship gave him to express himself on policy. The neat distinction between the diplomatic corps and the consular service never troubled him. Other British consuls in the United States shied from political and diplomatic questions; they bent over backward to confine themselves solely to economic affairs. Whenever driven to mention some political event, Sir John Temple inevitably begged the secretary of state's pardon for going "beyond the Consular Line of business." Never did Temple presume to offer an analysis of a diplomatic or political situation; for in his own words, "It would not become me to offer any opinion about them."[26]

Such reservations failed to cross Bond's mind. He filled his dispatches with descriptions of every aspect of American national life. He constantly told his government what they ought to do about various conditions. He never for long ceased to offer his own opinions, his own suggestions, and his own programs. The degree to which they affected policy is impossible to determine. Bond represented one of many sources of information available to the ministry. He was never in a position to make policy; he could only suggest and even in suggesting was overstepping the strict limitations of his office.

Still he exerted an influence. He helped convince the Lords of Trade that a commercial treaty with the United States would be beneficial. Without their acquiescence it is questionable whether the foreign department would have established diplomatic relations with America in 1791 and would have been prepared to discuss a commercial agreement. Some of his ideas found their way into the treaty and other ideas into the national law of Great Britain.

Certainly the dispatches set him apart from the other consuls in the United States and partly explained why the foreign department regarded Bond as their man there. His career also illustrated the inconsistencies in the department's position with respect to the service.

While the foreign office insisted upon the separation of diplomatic and consular functions,[27] they empowered Bond at the very beginning of his mission with two commissions, one consular and the other diplomatic; the latter was the commission of commissary for commercial affairs for all the United States. Had the Continental Congress accepted both credentials, Bond would have functioned in a dual capacity as consul and as minister of the second rank (see Chaps. IV and V).

Furthermore, throughout his career Bond reported directly to the secretary of state; to the same person to whom all British diplomats reported. By that procedure alone the two services tended to melt into one. In 1825, the foreign department finally admitted the contradiction inherent in that part of the system. They then created the office of superintendent of the consular service. Thereafter all British consuls addressed their dispatches to him.[28]

Bond regarded the two services as inseparable. Until his fall from grace with the unfortunate error over the Indian Treaty, he planned to move from the consular service into the diplomatic corps. But for that career he had opened the wrong door. In the eighteenth century, consuls seldom became ministers and ministers seldom rose from the ranks. They were usually outsiders: parliamentarians, statesmen, officers high in the armed services. The few career diplomats started, not as consuls, but generally as secretaries. Edward Thornton, who entered the corps as secretary of the legation under Hammond, had the key to preferment. He served in a temporary capacity as vice-consul at Baltimore. When Liston arrived, Thornton returned to his original post and from there gained one promotion after another. In 1811, while Bond was preparing for his final leave, Thornton was on his way to Sweden as His Majesty's minister plenipotentiary with special powers to negotiate a treaty of alliance.

The future vindicated Bond. After the war of 1939 the British foreign office abandoned the policy to which they clung for so long. At present the consular and diplomatic corps are merged in the British foreign service and officers move back and forth from ministerial to consular posts. Of that fusion Bond would thoroughly approve.

It would also have pleased him that at long last Philadelphians recognized his value as consul. The city never honored him while he lived. But when news arrived of his death, then the newspapers carried obituaries like the following which read in part:

> Faithful, zealous, and indefatigable in the discharge of his
> official duties, and performing with alacrity an extensive range of

gratuitous services, even to strangers, his incessant labors for the interests and accommodations of the public and of individuals gradually undermined an excellent constitution, and shortened a life valuable to his family, his friends, and the community at large.[29]

NOTES

[1]The traditional date for the origin of the consular service is 1485 when Richard III appointed Lorenzo Strozzi to be the British consul at Pisa.

[2]See Fair Copies of Commissions and Letters of Credence of Foreign Ministers and Consuls, 1778–1821, Item 129, on microfilm at the National Archives, Washington, D.C.

[3]See "Return of all the British Consuls and Vice-Consuls for the Year 1792 and 1821," *Accounts and Papers, British Sessional Papers* (London, 1822), XX, 79.

[4]George Aust to Bond, Downing Street, March 17, 1794, CAD COLL, PB, "Misc. Docs." Box.

[5]Lord Hawkesbury (1801–1804), Lord Harrowby (1804–1805), Lord Mulgrave (1805–1806), Charles James Fox (1806), Viscount Howick (1806–1807), George Canning (1807–1809), Earl Bathurst (1809), and the Marquis of Wellesley (1809–1812).

[6]Following his mission as minister to the United States George Hammond became, in 1795, under-secretary of state at the foreign department. He remained in that capacity until October 1809 when he retired to private life.

[7]Bond to Hammond, Philadelphia, October 12, 1804, Private, FO 5/43. For news about the embargo see, for instance, Bond to Hammond, Philadelphia, January 16, 1808 and May 5, 1808, FO 5/59.

[8]See Carmarthen to Bond, Whitehall, January 26, 1788 and December 4, 1789, FO 4/6, 4/7; Bond to Lord Hawkesbury, Rockwell, October 4, 1802 and order-in-council, April 5, 1804.

[9]See Bond to Grenville, Philadelphia, June 2, 1798, FO 5/23.

[10]See, for instance, Temple to Carmarthen, New York, October 4, 1786, FO 4/4; evidence of Joseph Henderson, consul general at Bogota before an investigating committee of the House of Commons, "Report from the Select Committee of Consular Establishment; Together with the Minutes of Evidence and Appendix," *British Sessional Papers* (London, 1835), VI, 170.

[11]Bond to Grenville, Philadelphia, January 6, 1795 and June 2, 1798, FO 115/4, 5/23.

[12]Bond to Grenville, Philadelphia, March 23, 1795, FO 115/4.

[13]Grenville to Bond, Whitehall, September 1791, FO 4/11.

[14]See, for instance, Liston's explanation that he owes Mr. Bond £315, Liston to Thomas Coutts, Philadelphia, April 13, 1797, Liston Mss.

[15]Edward Thornton, chargé d'affaires (1800–1803), Anthony Merry, minister plenipotentiary (1803–1806), David Montague Erskine, minister plenipotentiary (1806–1809), Francis James Jackson, minister plenipotentiary (1809–1810), John Philip Morier, chargé d'affaires (1810–1811), Augustus John Foster, minister plenipotentiary (1811–1812).

[16]Murray to Bond, Resolution at Sea, December 2, 1795, CAD COLL, PB, "Misc. Docs." Box.

[17]For Bond's program see Bond to Carmarthen, Philadelphia, February 21,

1787, *AHAAR,* 1896, I, 521–528; for the organization of the French and Dutch services see Fair Copes of Commissions and Letters of Credence of Foreign Ministers and Consuls, Item 129.

[18]Bond to Burges, Philadelphia, April 17, 1794, FO 5/6; Bond to Hammond, Philadelphia, September 24, 1796, Private, FO 115/4; Bond to Grenville, Philadelphia, April 3, 1798, FO 5/23.

[19]See especially Temple to Carmarthen, New York, April 7, 1786 and August 4, 1786, FO 4/4; Bond to Carmarthen, Philadelphia, August 3, 1786, *AHAAR,* 1896, I, 569–570; Bond to Leeds, July 28, 1789, FO 4/7; Hamilton to Leeds, Norfolk, May 25, 1791, FO 4/10; D. B. Horn, *The British Diplomatic Service, 1689–1789* (Oxford, 1961), Chap. XII. Salaries without fees proved unworkable; in 1825 parliament passed the first comprehensive consular act fixing fees and salaries, 6 Geo IV c. 87.

[20]For expenses see Temple to Carmarthen, New York, September 5, 1787, FO 4/5; for postage see, for instance, the testimony of Consul John Parkinson, Esq. "Report from the Select Committee of Consular Establishment," *BSP,* VI, 204 ff.

[21]Bond to Frazer, Philadelphia, October 1, 1787, *AHAAR,* 1896, I, 550–551.

[22]In 1801, for instance, a pound sterling equalled $4.75. When Timothy Pickering first became secretary of state he received $3,500 a year. In 1799, the salary was raised to $5,000. See Henry J. Ford, "Timothy Pickering, Secretary of State, December 10, 1795 to May 12, 1800," *Secretaries of State,* Samuel F. Bemis, ed. (New York, 1927–1928), II, 170.

[23]See Steward Irvin, *Consular Privileges and Immunities* (New York, 1926), *passim.*

[24]See, for instance, the invoices of William Blake for 1788 and of Thornton Mackaness for 1796, and the correspondence of Samuel Corp, 1798–1799, CAD COLL, PB, "Vouchers" and "Misc. Docs." Boxes.

[25]Bond to Canning, Philadelphia, July 14, 1807, FO 5/53.

[26]See, for instance, Temple to Carmarthen, New York, October 4, 1786, FO 4/4; Temple to Leeds, New York, March 10, 1791, FO 4/9.

[27]See the testimony of James Henderson and of William Keer Brown, "Report from the Select Committee of Consular Establishment," *BSP,* VI, 163 ff, 194 ff.

[28]6 Geo IV c 87.

[29]*Poulson's American Daily Advertiser* (Philadelphia, March 14, 1816), quoted by Edward Alfred Jones, *American Members of the Inns of Court* (London, 1924), p. 26.

Bibliography

Little has been written about Bond. No biography exists and there are no articles about him in the various biographical dictionaries. The following works mention him briefly:

Edward Alfred Jones *American Members of the Inns of Court* (London, 1924).

J. Thomas Schaf and Westcott Thompson *History of Philadelphia, 1609–1884* (Philadelphia, 1884). Confuses the doctor with the consul.

Wilbur H. Siebert *The Loyalists of Pennsylvania* (Columbus, 1905). Also confuses father and son.

Henry Simpson *The Lives of Eminent Philadelphians now Deceased Collected from Original and Authentic Sources* (Philadelphia, 1859).

As a result of the dearth of secondary material, the present study is based largely upon sources and especially upon Bond's official dispatches and the instructions sent to him. Published works:

Phineas Bond "Letters of Phineas Bond" J. Franklin Jameson, ed. *Annual Report of the American Historical Association for the Year 1896* (Washington, D.C., 1897) I, 513–659 and *Annual Report of the American Historical Association for the Year 1897* (Washington, D.C., 1898) 454–508. This work contains one hundred and two of Bond's letters for the years 1786 through 1793. In most instances the enclosures are omitted and the above, therefore, must be checked against the originals in the Public Record Office.

John Eardley-Wilmot *Historical View of the Commission for Enquiring into the Losses, Services, and Claims, of the American Loyalists, at the Close of the War Between Great Britain and her Colonies in 1783* (London, 1815).

Sophia Logan Fisher "A Diary of Trifling Occurrences, Philadelphia, 1776–1778" Nicholas Wainwright, ed. *Pennsylvania Magazine of History and Biography*, LXXXII (1958), 411–465.

Thomas Gilpin *Exiles in Virginia: With Observations on the Conduct of the Society of Friends During the Revolutionary War, Comprising the Official Papers of the Government Relating to that Period, 1777–1778* (Philadelphia, 1848). The most valuable printed source on Philadelphia Loyalists and their Virginian internment.

"Instructions to the British Ministers to the United States, 1791–1812" Bernard Mayo, ed. *Annual Report of the American Historical Association for the Year 1938* (Washington, D.C., 1941) III. Contains the instructions sent to Bond when he was chargé d'affaires.

Minutes of the Supreme Executive Council of Pennsylvania, from its Organization to the Termination of the Revolution XI, XV (1852).

Pennsylvania Archives, Selected and Arranged from Original Documents in the Offices of the Secretary of the Commonwealth

Samuel Hazard, ed. 1st Series, V, VI, XI (1853).

William Henry Egle, ed. 3rd Series, XIV, XXIV, XXVI (1897).

George Edward Reed, ed. 4th Series, III (1900).

Thomas Lynch Montgomery, ed. 6th Series, XII (1907).

Ann Warder "Extracts from the Diary of Ann Warder" Sarah Cadbury, ed. *Pennsylvania Magazine of History and Biography,* XVIII (1894), 51–63.

Unpublished documents in England:

Board of Trade. Public Record Office. BT 5/5, 6/20, 6/21, 6/22.

Burges Papers. Bodleian Library. At the time of writing this valuable collection remained uncatalogued.

Foreign Office. General Correspondence. America, United States. Public Record Office. FO 4/3 (1785), 4/4 (1786), 4/5 (1787), 4/6 (1788), 4/7 (1789), 4/8 (1790), 4/9 (1791), 4/10 (1791), 4/11 (1792), 4/14 (1792), 5/2 (1793), 5/6 (1794), 5/11 (1795), 5/13 (1795), 5/15 (1796), 5/19 (1797), 5/23 (1798), 5/26 (1799), 5/30 (1800), 5/33 (1801), 5/36 (1802), 5/39 (1803), 5/41 (1803), 5/43 (1804), 5/46 (1805), 5/50 (1806), 5/53 (1807), 5/59 (1808), 5/65 (1809), 5/71 (1810), 5/78 (1811), 5/89 (1812), 5/95 (1813), 5/100 (1814), 5/101 (1814), 5/108 (1815), 5/109 (1815). Contains over five hundred of Bond's letters, instructions to him, and dispatches from the other British consuls in the United States.

Loyalist Claims. Public Record Office. AO 12/38, 12/106, 13/70A.

Unpublished documents in the United States:

Dr. Thomas Bond and Dr. Phineas Bond Copartnership Day-books, 1751–July 1767. Library of the College of Physicians, Philadelphia.

British Foreign Correspondence: America, Henry Adams Transcripts. Hammond, 1789–1792. Library of Congress.

Cadwalader Collection. Phineas Bond and Thomas Bond Sections. Historical Society of Pennsylvania. This voluminous collection houses Bond's legal briefs, correspondence pertaining to cases, personal correspondence, family papers, financial accounts, and personal and household accounts.

Christ Church Records. Genealogical Society of Pennsylvania.

Clymer Mss. Historical Society of Pennsylvania.

Franklin Collection. American Philosophical Society, Philadelphia.

Gilbert Collection of Mss Letters. Library of the College of Physicians, Philadelphia.

Simon Gratz Collection. Historical Society of Pennsylvania. Phineas Bond Folder.

Misc. Mss. Collection. American Philosophical Society.

Peters Mss. Historical Society of Pennsylvania.

Rawle Papers. Historical Society of Pennsylvania.

Record of Deeds. County of Philadelphia. City Hall, Philadelphia. Books D2-12, 14, 17, 25, 30, 31, 34, 36, 40, 41, 42, 49; EF-24, 26, 30, 31, 32; I3-17; IC-9, 10, 11.

Yates Collection. Historical Society of Pennsylvania.

The British Consular Service

The history of the consular service in the reign of George III remains to be written. In its absence the following works proved the most useful:

"Account of the Estimate Charge of His Majesty's Civil List Revenues" *British Sessional Papers—Accounts and Papers,* VIII (1804), 849; XIII (1816), 17.

Violet Barbour "The Consular Service in the Reign of Charles II" *American Historical Review,* XXXIII (1928), 553–578.

S. T. Bindoff and E. F. Smith *British Diplomatic Representatives, 1789–1852* Camden 3rd Series L (London, 1934).

"An Estimate of the Sum which may be Wanted to Provide for the Salaries of His Majesty's Consuls General and Consuls

Abroad for the Year 1826" *British Sessional Papers,* XX (1826), 487.

Fair Copies of Commissions of Foreign Consuls, 1778–1785. National Archives, Washington, D.C. Available on microfilm.

Fair Copies of Commissions and Letters of Credence of Foreign Ministers and Consuls, 1778–1821. National Archives, Washington, D.C. Available on microfilm.

Robert Fynn *British Consuls Abroad: Their Origin, Rank and Privileges, Duties, Jurisdiction and Emoluments: Including the Laws, Orders in Council, and Instructions by which They are Governed, as well as Those Relating to Ship-Owners and Merchants in Connection with Consuls* (2nd ed. London, 1849). This is the first consular handbook in the English language.

D. B. Horn *The British Diplomatic Service, 1689–1789* (Oxford, 1961). An excellent study with several very useful chapters on consuls and consulates.

"Minutes of Evidence Taken before the Committee of the Whole House, to whom it was Referred to Consider if the Several Petitions which had been Presented to the House, in this Session of Parliament, Relating to the Orders in Council" *British Sessional Papers,* III (1812), 1–900.

"Return of all the British Consuls and Vice-Consuls Abroad for the Year 1792 and 1821" *British Sessional Papers, Accounts and Papers,* XX (1822), 79.

"Report from the Select Committee of Consular Establishment; Together with the Minutes of Evidence, and Appendix" *British Sessional Papers,* VI (1835), 149–255.

E. W. A. Tuson *The British Consul's Manual: Being a Practical Guide for Consuls as well as the Merchant, Ship-owner and Master Mariner in all their Consular Transactions* (London, 1856).

Emerich de Vattel *The Law of Nations, or Principles of the Law of Nature Applied to the Conduct and Affairs of Nations and Sovereigns,* Joseph Chitty, ed. (Philadelphia, 1859).

A. de Wicquefort *The Embassador and his Functions,* Trans. John Digby (London, 1716).

More attention has been paid to the American consular service than to the British. The following American studies proved helpful:

Stewart Irvin *Consular Privileges and Immunities* (New York, 1926). Although weighted on the American service, this is a very useful work.

Luke T. Lee *Consular Law and Practice* (New York, 1961). An authoritative treatment of the services of all modern nations.

Graham H. Stuart *American Diplomatic and Consular Practice* (New York, 1936). The classic work on the subject.

Charles W. Thayer *Diplomat* (New York, 1959).

Associates of Bond

There are no biographies of the two secretaries of state with whom Bond was most closely associated, Leeds and Grenville. The latter, in particular, deserves a full-length study.

Oscar Browning, ed. *The Political Memoranda of Francis, Fifth Duke of Leeds* (Westminster, 1884). The introduction offers the best available sketch of the secretary.

Historical Manuscripts Commission. *The Manuscripts of the Duke of Leeds* 11th Report, Appendix, Part VII. (London, 1888).

Historical Manuscripts Commission. *Report on the Manuscripts of J. B. Fortesque, Esq. Preserved at Dropmore.* These are the Grenville papers, but unfortunately they contain only meager references to Bond and to American affairs in general.

For the British ministers to the United States see in particular:

Samuel Flagg Bemis *Jay's Treaty, A Study in Commerce and Diplomacy* (New York, 1924). Treats Hammond's mission in considerable detail.

A. L. Burt *The United States, Great Britain and British North America from the Revolution to the Establishment of Peace after the War of 1812* (New Haven, 1941).

Alexander DeConde *Entangling Alliance: Politics and Diplomacy under George Washington* (Durham, N.C., 1958). An excellent study.

Liston Manuscripts. National Library of Scotland, Edinburgh. Acc. No. 720, Boxes XII-XIV. Available on microfilm from the Library of Congress.

Bradford Perkins *The First Rapprochement, England and the United States, 1795–1805* (Philadelphia, 1955). A thorough work particularly useful for Liston's mission.

Bradford Perkins *Prologue to War, England and the United States, 1805–1812* (Berkeley, 1961). The best correlation and synthesis of the causes of the War of 1812.

Leslie Reade "George III to the United States Sendeth Greeting. . . ." *History Today VIII* (November 1958), 770–780. A lively account of Hammond's tour.

Beckles Willson *Friendly Relations, A Narrative of Britain's Ministers and Ambassadors to America, 1791–1930* (Boston, 1934).

Esmond Wright "Robert Liston, Second British Minister to the United States." *History Today XI* (February 1961), 118–127.

For Bond's consular colleagues, in addition to the invaluable dispatches in the foreign office collection in the Public Record Office, the following proved helpful:

Thomas Barclay *Selections from the Correspondence of Thomas Barclay, Formerly British Consul-General At New York,* George Lockhard Rives, ed. (New York, 1894).

Bowdoin and Temple Papers, Collections of the Massachusetts Historical Society. 7th Series, VI (1907).

Lewis Einstein *Divided Loyalties, Americans in England During the War for Independence* (London, 1933). Contains an interesting chapter on Sir John Temple.

The Gentleman's Magazine and Historical Chronicle. Invaluable source for tracing secondary figures.

Historical Manuscripts Commission. *The Manuscripts of the Earl of Dartmouth* II (1895).

Robert O. DeMond *The Loyalists in North Carolina During the Revolution* (Durham, N.C., 1940). Describes consul Hamilton's activities during the war.

Sir Edward Thornton Memoirs. Manuscript Division, Library of Congress.

For an evaluation of Bond's influence upon the government, the following works were the most important:

International Adjudications Ancient and Modern, John Bassett Moore, ed. III, IV (New York, 1931).

Journals of the House of Commons, XXXIX, XL (1803).

The Parliamentary Debates, Thomas C. Hansard, ed. I–VIII (1803–1807).

The Parliamentary History of England, William Cobbett, ed. XXII–XXV (1814).

"Report from the Committee on the Survey of the Coasts of Scotland Relating to Emigration" *British Sessional Papers,* IV (1802–1803), 1–38.

Report of a Committee of the Privy Council on the Trade of Great Britain with the United States, January 1791 Worthington C. Ford, ed. (Washington, D.C., 1888).

Statutes at Large.

Statutes of the Realm.

James Fulton Zimmerman *Impressment of American Seamen* (New York, 1925).

Other primary and secondary sources used in preparing this work may be found in the author's manuscript entitled, His Britannic Majesty's Consul General, Phineas Bond, Esq. at the Bryn Mawr College Library and on microfilm at the University of Michigan in Ann Arbor.

INDEX

Act for the Increase and Encouragement of Shipping and Navigation, 42, 44, 50 n. 7
Active, ship, 110
Adams, Charles Francis, 145 n. 5
Adams, John, 6, 34, 38 n. 4, 68
Addington, Henry, 148
Admiralty, 163
Adventure, passenger ship, 149
Africa, British warship, 119 n. 24, 136
Allen family, 4, 54, 110
Allen, Andrew, 110
Allen, Margaret, 110
American Philosophical Society, 4, 9
Ames, Esther, 64 n. 9
Anderson, James Pettit, 54
Anglo-American relations, summarized, xi-xii; American reaction to PB's appointment, 5-7, 46-49; states contravene peace treaty, 25-26; growing distrust, 27-28; Britain willing to negotiate commercial treaty with U. S., 78; British minister appointed, 79; American minister appointed, 86; Jefferson's memorial on British contravention of peace treaty, 87-88; Hammond and PB's countermemorial, 88-89; Jefferson's counter countermemorial, 91-93; effect of war with France on, see France; and impressment, 95-96, 130, 151-152; and citizenship, 96, 152; British consuls become spies, 99; Anglophobia, 101-102, 114-115; *Jane* affair, 111-112; *Daedalus* affair, 115-116; American neutrality preserved by commercial treaty, 116, 118, 122; Randolph problem, 122, 134-136;

British seizure of American ships, 130-131; American people opposed to treaty, 130-132; opposition continues after ratification, 134; *Africa* incident, 136; Treaty of Greenville, 139-140, 142-143; Treaty of Amity confirmed by Congress, 142; begin to improve, 143. See also Merchants, Migration, Northwest posts, Trade, Treaty of Amity.
Annapolis Convention, 43-44
Antigua, 106
Argyle, Duke of, 150
Asylum for Fugitive Pieces, 4
Aust, George, 84, 94, 118, 137, 157
Ayres, Captain, 13

Bache, Benjamin Franklin, 128
Bacheran, Andrew, 119 n. 20
Bacheran, George, 119 n. 20
Ball, Lady, 157
Baltimore, 116
Barclay family, 157
Barclay, Robert, 29 n. 14, 33, 69, 81, 83, 98
Barclay, Thomas, 143, 144
Barney, Captain Joshua, 116
Bartram, John, 9
Bathurst, Earl, 175 n. 5
Beckwith, George, 87
Bemis, Samuel Flagg, 7 n. 8, 38 n. 4, 99 n. 20, 176 n. 22
Bermuda, 117
Biddle, Charles, 46, 51 n. 20
Biddle, Henry D., 64 n. 9
Bingham family, 54
Bird, Dolly & Co., 29 n. 14